Acclaim for *In My Own Voice*

This unusual collection of well-wrought, deeply felt poems, covering a forty-year span of a woman's life, becomes a kind of poetic autobiography. Registering all along the scale of emotion, her poems treat subjects that range from the awakening of sexual love, to a beloved child's incurable illness, to the joy of just being alive in our moment on earth, to helping parents die, to the onset of the weaknesses that come with one's own aging. This work transcends the personal to explore the tragedy, as well as the saving humor, of the human condition. This poet's eye is sharp, her heart is wide awake, and her poems speak truths we sometimes know but don't stop to articulate. Her book is a blessing, an affirmation of a life heartily relished.

Jane Gentry Vance, Kentucky Poet Laureate;
Professor, University of Kentucky; Author

⁊०

Many careful people keep diaries; a few write poems. Barbara Mabry has chronicled her life and what was and is important in it in this impressive collection of poems. Her verses project images and thoughts and sentiments from times past: vivid flashes of memory of her parents, young and old; her husband; the birth and growth of her children; a sermon that holds her accountable; country sayings that make sense through generations; a day of scudding clouds and flowers and love; dogs; owls; phoebes and bluebirds; a war memorial; their mountain hideaway; aging; memorable people who are admirable, odd, or foolish; time; gingko leaves; joy and sorrow; the merging of past and present; the living and the dead; and hope. There is much more, too, in well-chosen words, buttressed by haunting photographs artfully screened behind her poems. Barbara Mabry has spoken to, as well as for, all of us in this book.

– Loyal Jones, retired director of the Berea College Appalachian Center; Author

⁊०

The real subject of Barbara Mabry's In My Own Voice is the impulse to metaphor, the persistence of poem-making in the life of a singular woman—wife and mother, teacher and caregiver, but always, too, a writer. Her book chronicles that life in a patchwork of poetry. Sturdier and more studied than the "scrapbook" the poet modestly calls the volume, this quilt is broad and varied, each poem raising a person or moment, place or memory as shaped in the mind of the poet. It is clear that these poems companioned Mabry through the forty years of their making. With the publication of this rich body of work, Barbara Mabry will surely be remembered as "a maker of poems."

– Leatha Kendrick, Poet; Author; Teacher

Varied in tone, subject, and setting, Mabry's poems give us what she calls "a field trip" of her life--from girlhood to retirement, from ancestors to grandchildren. They take us to the holy stones of Iona and to her own retreat at Sourwood Hollow, asking the heart's deep questions.

– GeorgeElla Lyon, Poet; Author; Teacher

ℬ

In the last poem of this richly varied collection, the author, Barbara Mabry, muses about how she might be remembered. She notes that, among other things, she wouldn't mind being remembered as a planter of trees, or a grower of fruit, or even a wind watcher and then casually adds, almost as an afterthought, as "a maker of poems." Anyone who reads these poems will wholeheartedly agree that, as Emily Dickinson once put it, "This was a poet."

Out of the disparate crowded materials of her life as daughter, mother, wife, editor, teacher and writer Barbara Mabry has honed poems that are in her own words, "straightforward, informal, transparent and accessible." More than that, though, her poems have their own distinctive voice; one that is acutely observant of the natural world; one that lyrically recreates the mysteries of the passing seasons; and one that probes deeply into "the layered hard packed years" to unearth both "artifacts/and majestic ruins/ of my former selves." At the center of her life and this collection reside her quest for meaning and her role as a "knocker on doors/ who goes on knocking/even when no one ever answers." In her poems she faces unflinchingly the hard questions of old age, faith, death and loss and brings to these eternal problems insights filled with wisdom and humor as well as hard won realism.

Yet these poems are neither tracts nor philosophic discussions, but rather lyrical narratives and reflective musings that both surprise and delight the reader with their keen human insights and sensuous reminders of the human condition. And poems demonstrate her gifts for apt metaphor and graphic detail: So a baby's delicate fingers are depicted as "furled like fern fronds, our own springtime's bud;" a determined eighty three year old working in her garden to eradicate bugs and beetles "tolerates hard-baked dirt /no better than impervious minds;" gentle ladies in a nursing home are seen as "bunches of dried flowers/withered, papery, faded;" the Christian cross's form indicates its symbolic significance, being without "soft edges," and having "Blunt ends, right angles,/ splinters./ It is meant to kill;" and visiting the Vietnam War Memorial on a hot summer day encloses one in "the moist rice-paddy heat" and the "dark embrace" of "bright-polished/tapering black-granite wings."

It's difficult to select favorites from the abundance given in this collection of over 200 poems, but "Crops" works magic with the stones turned up in spring plowing. In "Punishment" a girlhood memory of being disciplined with willow switches evolves into a humorous yet poignant story of an ongoing mother-daughter conflict. "Ubi Est" evokes the breathtaking image of a long-legged, knobby-kneed colt of a girl, running barefoot "along the sharp-edged/slanted rocks/ atop the stacked rock fence" to show off for her older cousins. "A Craving Woman" cleverly chronicles the desires of a country wife who craves until she is about to be buried, while "Highway Ten Twenty-Eight" graphically depicts the strange mixture of natural growth, litter and poverty-stricken life that fill the countryside.

The book is divided thematically into sections like "Journeys" which mainly confronts matters of faith and belief; and"Portraits From Life" and "Stories," which narrate country tales and anecdotes from farm life. Another section, called "Musings," offers cryptic, ironic comments on life and its foibles like "Old Dogs," which remarks that "old dogs/ trying to learn/ new tricks/ are fun/ to be around." Another entitled "Fatal Attraction" comments that the writer has always cherished "a secret desire/ to be fatally attractive/ to someone other than/ old men,/little boys,"/…and dogs." Finally "Commonplace Puddles" notes that for most people these areas are not "deep enough/to drown in/ but quite sufficient/to muddy us up."

One other visual pleasure found in this volume is its use of old black and white photographs from the author's collection scattered throughout at appropriate times to both supplement and complement the poems themselves. So, for example, "Homeplace" ends with a photograph of a log cabin in winter, while "Sheep" features a photograph of sheep crossing a road as a backdrop for the poem

Perhaps the climax of the collection is a grouping called "Sourwood And Other Loves" where thirty-four poems evoke the seasonal progression from spring to winter as viewed from the vantage point of old pioneer cabin in the Kentucky hills. Here the descriptions of an old barn, a black-velvet bee, a small country creek, the leaves of October, the cutting down of an old peach tree, and a winter landscape offer the reader an imagistic invitation into the secret places where the soul finds sanctuary and healing spaces. One of its poems, "Riches to Rags," quietly displays the treasures that the whole collection offers:

> All summer through, the hills,
>   like prosperous burghers,
> waxed plump and sleek.
>   They clustered round
>   The hollow's rim—
>   gregarious.
> Now in mid-December,
>   the ridges stand separate, aloof,
> withdrawn, as poor men stand,
>   ribs and backbones showing,
>   quivering in the winds,
>   their summer finery
> in tatters at their feet.

— Ben Pickard, Professor, University of Florida; Author; Editor

In My Own Voice

Poems
1967 - 2007

Barbara Mabry

The Clark Group

Lexington, Ky.
2007

ISBN 978-1-883589-81-3

Book design and composition by Kelly Elliott

Cover design by Amanda K. Nedley

To Charlton -- helpmate, partner, best friend, soul-match, husband. I am blessed with our long and lovely love.

Acknowledgements

This book is a sort of miracle-in-the-making. I am grateful to so many: to Anne Gabbard, Ann Fister, and Matt McMahan, who typed many, many poems to get them into my computer; to Florence Huffman, my publisher/editor at The Clark Group, who believed in me and my work; to Kelly Elliott, who, with patience, did the hard work of lay-out; to Bobby Clark and Sam Stephens also at Clark--all of whom wanted to make this happen; to my husband Chart for his patience and constant helpfulness; to my parents, Leo and Louvenia Blum for my loving, stable, and rich tail-end-of-Depression childhood; to all our children, especially Jonathan (who critiqued), Anne, who encouraged, and grandchildren, who are subjects, of course; to friends who have urged and encouraged over the years; to poets whose work I have read over a lifetime; to long-ago teachers: Esther Mae Ayres, Carolyn Blair, Edwin R. Hunter, Elizabeth Jackson. To numerous friends who are published poets--for their example, teaching, and helpful commentary along the way. And to UK students who told me I "opened up" poetry for them; and gratitude for all the people and places I observed, listened to, absorbed, imagined, loved, and wrote about. And especially for Mike and Helen Mabry, who put me in touch with Amanda K. Nedley of Pittsburgh, a talented graphic artist who is responsible for the lovely and personally meaningful cover art.

Table of Contents

PERSPECTIVE

PORTRAITS FROM LIFE

STORIES

ODDITIES

Sourwood And Other Loves

Foreword

In My Own Voice is almost an anthology or maybe a scrapbook, but it is my own voice, of course, strengthened and defined over nearly three-quarters of a century—settling in as straightforward, informal, transparent, and accessible. It has come a long way, for I started writing at least by age six, when the *Knoxville News Sentinel* published a small poem of mine about fairies. When I was ten, they published another. During the summers I was the sole copywriter at the largest radio station in Knoxville, Tennessee (writing 17 beer commercials a day one summer for Game of the Day). I also learned to run the console, so that, in college, I could air our programs on the Maryville College station. I wrote a play for our high school senior drama and another for college production. I taught radio speech and dramatics in a plush office on the top floor of the City Hall in Atlanta, Georgia (and worked my way down ever after). After moving around the country for my husband's training, I began teaching at the University of Kentucky when our youngest child started school.

Early on, however, I was jotting down bits of poems and thinking, thinking, but marriage, work, and graduate school (I was the first woman to hold a full scholarship at Emory University), then four babies in six years--all conspired to silence my poetic typewriter. But always, wherever we moved, whatever situation I was in, I was writing--or editing. I edited my husband's medical journal articles, literary magazines, a math book, a chemistry book, journals, a gardening magazine, many scientific books and articles; wrote church histories, sketches, memoirs, articles. But Poetry came bubbling to the top by the sixties and found itself percolating along by the eighties; I enjoyed and profited from writer-friends, workshops, and submissions--and reading poetry. I learned while teaching good literature at the University. I learned from the students I taught, watched, advised; I grew with them and was enriched by them. Writing has helped to sustain me, so far, through chronic illnesses of two of our children--as has gardening. The quest and need for love and beauty--and continued growth--and tolerance for differences--are about all I have come to feel that I understand in this life. I have always, always been fascinated by the infinite human variety in this world we inhabit. There is so much more that we will never know or experience--or witness. For each, there is just our own slice.

I began to send poems in to literary journals and joyed in seeing my work in print. But most of all, I wrote for myself; it was really not frequent before the last decade that I shared my poems with friends and did a few readings. It has been like coming out of the closet and more than a little scary to think of unknown people reading my selection of poems from a life's collection. (You will be able to tell early poems from later.) And exciting. And terrifying. A poem, as you may know, takes on a life of its own, so that often the ending or the direction it takes is a surprise to the poet. Poems collect in file drawers and folders until they have a weight that demands the light of readership. So, at my age, (and with full file drawers), I did not want to gamble on successive smaller books. When the offer of publication came, I thought it must be all in one volume, just in case time ran out. The photographs are mine, too, with no thought for publication, so they are also homely and significant to me. The drawing on page 142 is by my son, Jonathan. Now that these poems are going to be "set in stone," I can think of so many more I want and need to write.

— Barbara Mabry   May 6, 2007

ALONG THE WAY

FIELD TRIP

More than half a century
    we have spent
meshing our metaphors,
    blending our bodies,
growing together--
    souls and minds.
So when he says my efforts
    at putting a book of poems
            together
remind him of a field trip--
    well, not the trip,
but the paper you write
    about it to turn in,
I laugh but listen up.
        But, he says,
this is not just any trip--
    no, it is special--
it is our lives' field trip
    you are writing about--
compiling and refining
            to turn in,
It is a metaphor
    to blow my mind.
We have made
so many metaphors,
        we two--
four of them
    live and two-legged.

And now this.

A PRIVATE THING

&

I had fully intended,
when I sat down
to write a poem today,

to set down thoughts and words

as vigorous as kudzu,
as inevitable as sumac,
as showy as ironweed.

But when I reached inside
to draw them out,
I found something

as fragile as a mud-and-moss
phoebe's nest perched
on the cabin's doorframe,

as chancey as pearls
strung on a cotton thread,

as quivery as tears held back.

And I wondered if I dared
to write such a private thing.

POEMS LURKING

Somewhere,
among the thick grass
and matted underbrush
    of my mind,
there are poems lurking--
    hiding like meadow-larks,
startling at my approach
    and flying up in frantic haste
to evade my capture.

I have given up hope
    of stumbling upon
any nest-sitting birds.

THIS, TOO, QUICKENS

This, too, quickens,
this live poem
   within me.
Conceived long ago
   in innocence, in recognition,
      it rises unbidden,
drawing its sustenance,
   taking form and shape.
Now it quickens,
   flutters,
becomes throbbing force,
   demands
            to be delivered
                     alive.

MIXED EMOTIONS

The thrill is for

the sleep-blushed

curve of his cheek,

the pang for

the tender flesh

at the nape of his neck,

the leap of the heart

for the eager innocent eyes

and the outstretched trusting hands,

the chill

for his mutability.

For Adam Charlton

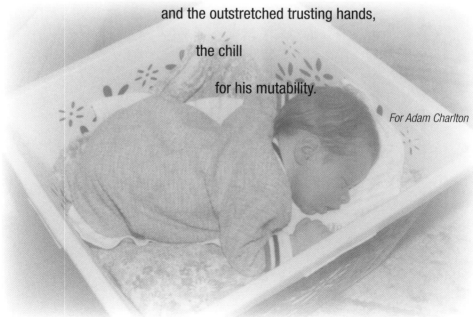

A STAR FOR YOUR HAND

&

I reach down,
and he reaches up
to clasp my fingers.
In such a way we bridge
  the generation gap.
We walk over new-green grass;
we savor new sweet sunlight
and prance with new shadows.
Hear bee, he says,
  and we do.
Smell flowers, he says,
  and we do.
Sun pretty, he says--
  where star?
He reaches up his hand
to me, to the sky.
  Oh, my dear little new one,
  I would put in
        your hand a star
              if I could.

for Adam

BRIAN

You came in early
   blossom time--
in lilac and
   wild-plum blossom time--
before redbud,
   before dogwood,
      before leaf-time.

You were soft-pink
   and gold,
winsome as the most
   delicate new green.

Expected and
   as longed for
as the springtime,
   you came as fresh
as the new-old
   vernal wakening,
as the green breath
   over the land.

You are our blossom,
   our tender opening bud,
      our soft-unfurling leaf,
      our unspoken hope.

We shall watch
   you tremulously,
wonder at
   the glory
of your unfolding
   to this new world--
         of our dreaming,
            of your blossoming.

FOR ANDREW, UNIQUE

It doesn't matter that
        you are only the latest one
of numberless-forever babies
        or that you are
the third of three for us –
        for you are the first
                of you.
You are a snowflake,
        unique forever,
or a curled leaf-bud
        with your little furled ears,
the faint cleft in your chin,

and your miniature fingernails.
There has been none
        just like you, ever before,
nor will there ever be again.
        We move you at once
into the new room
        we have made for you
in our hearts, our lives,
        and you yawn and squeak,
stretch, wiggle, and blink,
        snuggle down
        as if you know
that you have come home
        to us at last – to us
who have been waiting
        just for you.

We will tell you some day,
        how you came early,
        in the winter snow,
and brought a new spring
        with you.

I WANT YOU TO KNOW

&

I want you to know:
   there was a full maternal moon
laying down a princely path of silver
   the night that you were born.
And when the glad news came
   on that pristine May morning,
   gold-spattered bees were sipping
pink-lavender from wild phlox
   on the hillsides above the cabin,
and the woods were alive and bright
   with birdsong for your heralding.
Dogwood blossoms were a froth
   of christening-white
amid new-greening woods.
   It was all new for you.

Spring came late to us this year;
   perhaps reserving
      its glory, its fullness,
         my little one--
                  waiting for you.

for Alan Joseph Mabry

MOON-APPLE

ॐ

Today we picked
the last of the apples.
   Now tonight,
in his tall father's arms,
   he tries to pick
September's high white moon.

Hair moon-silvered,
   he stretches out his hand;
his father holds him up, up
   (from where I stand,
his fingertips brush the moon).

   Can't reach it, he says--
it's too high up--
   we better get the ladder!

   Toward morning,
I dream he picks
   the silver-apple moon
and brings it to me,
   holding it in front of him
      like a shield.
But I can see right through it
   to his luminous small face.

   I wanted to give you
a moon for each hand,
      he says.

And I reach out to receive it,
      thinking
         and I never have even
               wished
      for the moon.

NOSEGAY FOR RACHEL

You with the petal face--
you open virginal eyes
upon an ancient earth
refurbished now with blossoms.
It is fitting that you have come to us
when seasons have turned again
toward green and flowering hope.
You are, with your delicate fingers
furled like fern fronds,
our own springtime's bud,
our own puissant prophet
speaking with spring-soft lips
of seedtime once again
and promise of fruit to come.
You sleep, unaware
that blackberries froth
in fountain-sprays along fence rows
or that wild roses shake
pale petals in the breeze,
or that locusts yield heavy flowerets
to the questing bee.

I could press and save for you
these birth mementos,
but now I pick instead
a fresh and welcoming
nosegay
of hope and peace and love--
fragrant and fragile
as joy.

RIDING-THUNDER DREAMS
&

He paints his world
    from a palette
of fresh-mixed words;
    My daddy--he's 'way high up;
shh--listen… I hear a purple train!
    And…someday, someday,
Adam will ride the thunder--
        thunder's *big*!

I hope, my little one,
you can keep your
    riding-thunder dreams.

THE QUESTION

What are these,
  he asks, pointing
to the big pan
  of red steamed crabs.
Crabs your granddaddy--
  and you helped--
caught this morning,
  remember, with the string
and chicken necks and net.
  No, he says,
stabbing his finger
  at me and frowning.
Crabs downstairs outside
  in the basket--
crabs green and
  they have pinch-fingers
and they wiggle.
  What are these?
he asks, insisting.
  His eyes are wary now.
Not crabs,
  he says,
    Not.

IN THIS ONLY DAY

There is so much joy
in the finding,
perhaps you'll never know
when you are lost,
and so I'll not show,
my own little boy,
not show you the cost,
the art of the winding.

SPARKS

We are out on the cabin's dog-trot,
    reveling in the coming storm,
watching the lashing of the trees,
    listening to the growling thunder
and the brisk thrum of the rain
        on the old tin roof.
He has never seen lightning
    so brilliant, so raw, so close.
When it splits the sky, he says,
    "Oh, Nana, did you see--
sparks flew through the air--
    did you see them--
        and set the rain on fire!"

Together we feel the thunder
    roll around the hollow
while sparks fly through our air.

DON'T FORGET DANDELIONS
&

In this his fourth spring
  we are talking robins
and worms and greening grass,
  daffodils and redbuds and dogwoods.
"Now don't forget dandelions,
  Nana," he warns,
"and violets. Remember?"
  I, who have been doggedly
digging out, eliminating,
  dandelions and violets,
answer him--regretfully now:
  "Adam, I don't have any dandelions.
Perhaps you'll save me some?"
  "No dandelions?" he asks,
pitying me, wondering
  how this had happened.
"Don't worry, Nana,
  I'll find you some.
You need some dandelions."
  "I'm lucky to have you
to look after me," I tell him,
  remembering dandelion crowns
and clover-chain necklaces
  and violet nosegays
in tiny cream bottles.

BOY ON A TRACTOR

At barely two,
  he sits atop his grandfather's
twenty-year-old Massey-Ferguson
  and pretends to drive it.
He has clambered up
  with tremendous effort
and feels great pride
  that he has achieved this seat.
Now he pours the gasoline in
  and reaches for the key to turn it on.
He jiggles the gears
  and turns the steering wheel
a few inches, back and forth.
  At home, back in the city,
he has talked about this big red tractor
  frequently and earnestly,
and he greets it with shouts of joy.
  His little world is marvelously expanded
by the elderly red tractor,
  and he is the undoubted lord
of all that he surveys.
  His size and strength
are multiplied by this connection
  of his hands upon this steering wheel.
The wind blows his blonde hair
  back from his face
and his eyes shine.
  His speed just sitting still
propels him full-tilt
  into sweet-clovered fields
of childhood's memories.

SANDPILE STANDOFF

ॐ

They sit together this sultry summer
   early morning--little brown-gold boy
in the sand box and grandfather
   sitting with his back against the shed.
He pours sand with an old teapot,
   making miniature anthills.
The sand clings to his moist skin.
   Grandfather plays with a plastic bat.
He leans over and pours sand
      onto the grass.
"Keep it in the sandbox, Alan."
   Alan fills the pot slowly, carefully,
and pours it slowly into the grass.
   "No," grandfather says, and taps
      him with the bat.
Alan fills and pours;
   grandfather taps gently at first,
      then a little harder.
Alan studies him carefully.
   Neither drops his eyes.
Alan fills the pot and
   pours the sand on the edge,
so that half trickles over the side.
   Grandfather taps him with the bat.
Alan fills the pot, holds it up;
   Grandfather raises the bat.
Then Alan throws his head back
   and laughs---stands up and laughs,
      They laugh together
      in the hot July sun.

SERVICE STATION

&

Our house
    is a service station.
They drive through
    only to fill up.
        get washed,
use the restroom,
    take a quick nap--
before driving
        off
to private, urgent
    adolescent rendezvous.

The attendants
    get no tips.

SCHOOL VACATION

Carpet treads
        worn,
toilet seat
        chipped,
refrigerator shelves
        sticky and bare,
laundry hamper
        reeking,
and beds
        ravaged.

The children are all
home again this summer.

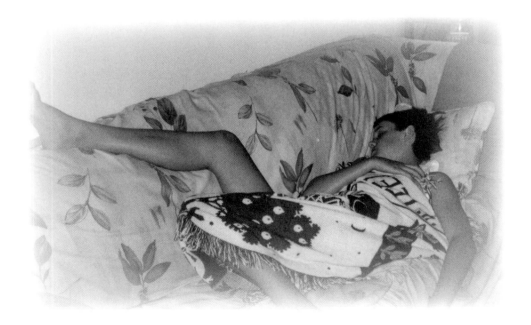

MIDNIGHT CINDERELLA
&

I wish his car
would turn into a pumpkin
   at the stroke of twelve
and her jeans to tatters--
   a midnight Cinderella.
She needs no fairy godmother
   to dazzle her handsome prince.
But I, a wicked stepmother,
   awake as the clock strikes one,
fret in my bed
   as the murmuring
        goes on
          and on.
At last she shuts the door
      behind him
and climbs the darkened staircase,
   lit by her glass-slipper glow.

LETTING GO

Is hard,
and there is no help for it.

I remember the time
you climbed up to the high board
and stood at the end
looking down at the water

so far below.
You were so small,
    afraid
of the unknown plunge--
and I wanted to call you
    back then, too.
But you held your breath
    and jumped--
splatted the water
    and sank,
then came up grinning--
    triumphant.

I hope this letting go
will be

    a floating down,
a merging, and

    a rising.

WHETHER THE HEARTS

The clocks tick,
   the hearts beat,
and time moves on--
   whether the hearts
are breaking.

Hands touch,
   eyes tear,
and hours pass--
   whether the hearts
can bear the hope
   of miracle
in the making.

This too--
   the clocks tick,
the hearts beat--
   shall pass.
There is today
   and a possible
tomorrow.

HOSTAGE

૪૭

He sees each day's headlines
   blaring news of hijackers
and hostages in Iran.

He translates to himself:
  I am a hostage
to this disease
   that no one understands--
neither cause nor cure.
   I am hostage
to uncertainty
   and unpredictability--
a random victim of hijacking
   and a senseless ravishing
of mind and body.
   And for me--
for me--a hostage also,
   there is no ransom.

     He tries to be glad
     when they are freed.

THIS PEACE,

&

He said,
   I leave with you;
my peace I give to you…

  and I will take it
    hungrily,
  as a wafer laid
    upon the tongue
to dissolve, warming
    brain and blood,
like sacramental wine.
  And I would pass
    this peace to you
  that you may be
    filled with peace

    and move,

    somehow bodiless,

    lightly

    into the light.

JOURNEYS

RACHELS WEEPING

&

An incredible story:
  born in a stable,
laid in a manger,
  gloried by a single star,
worshipped by shepherds
  and wise men alike,
lulled by mother's crooning,
  and cradled in father's arms,
lapped round by the singing
    of angels--
Jesus the Christ.

But there are other players
  in the story:
Herod the paranoid, fearful king--
  and the soldiers he sent
to kill all the babies
  in Bethlehem,
and the families
  who had no angel
to warn them
  to take their babies
    and flee to Egypt's safety,
    as Joseph had.

So let it be remembered
  that there were sounds
other than singing and celebration:
  the wailing of mothers
    of butchered babies--

lamentation keening through the joy--
  soul-searing sounds
    of Rachels weeping
for their precious children
  because they were no more.

Exultation, then, muted with tears,
  and prophecies fulfilled--
the long road to the cross begun,
  leaving behind a star, a stable,
the Rachels and their sacrifice.
  Rachels weeping, unconsoled.

SILENCE

The silence at the center
   daunts me
    taunts me.
 I have been promised
   something is there.
Not a burning bush maybe--
no mountain-top tablets,
   but a hair-counter,
   a sparrow watcher,
    an answerer when I call.

I have been told
it is never too late
   to seek,
that unworthiness
   doesn't matter,
that there is grace
   enough for all.

And so the inward spiral,
   the reverberating fear,
the suspicion
   that most likely
    the void is me,
that faith is really hope,
   who speaks in a human voice.

So I am a knocker on doors
   who goes on knocking
even when no one ever answers--

a wind-watcher,
who still tries to net the wind--
a dreamer of brave dreams
   who knows they are dreams,
one who faces the aloneness--
   the awful silence at the core,

...and goes on listening,
            listening

EDGES
&

There are no soft edges
   to the cross.
Blunt ends, right angles,
   splinters.

It is meant to kill.

The cross does not conform,
   not cradle,
      not comfort.

And the way of the cross
   is hard:
uncompromising,
   unyielding,
merciless.

The shadow of the cross
   falls over us,
each of us,
   brands us
with its hard edges,
   wounds us.

Hard edges cut,
   are costly,
life-changing,
   demanding.

We shift against the edges,
  try to find a place
of comfort.
  Even cross-shadows
penetrate.

But

then there were no Easter edges

at

Golgotha.

STAR-STRUCK

Oh, Lord, one more time,
let me be glory-smitten--
     star-struck--
be-dazzled and bewildered
     by miracle.
Let relentless star-shine
strike deep down
     into my black abyss
of doubt and cynicism--
my fear of age and war
     and terror--
transfix, transmute
     with splendor
     of simple Gift
     and Giver.
Oh, Lord, one more time--
     star-struck.

A SILENT NIGHT

A silent night there was
   before the celebration--
a single brighter star
   before the angels sang.
A holy hush there was
   before the jubilation--
a tiny babe straw-cradled
   before the labored climb
            to Golgotha.
An humble human joy there was
   before the cry of Savior, King--
a long and silent time
   before the revelation:
            He was our God come down;
            only after the cross, the crown.

Or so the story goes.

SPARROWS FALLING

Sparrows are falling
   all around--
there, but here, too
   in Somalia
   in Bosnia
   in Darfur
   on Maxwell Street
   on Albany Road
   and East Seventh Street.
Sparrows are falling
   now, and will tomorrow.

Is the great, good God
   marking their fall
   cupping His hands
   spreading His wings
to stop the carnage,
   to cushion the pain?
Or does He send instead
   His winged minions, His angels,
and are they too overworked
   to do anything
    about the sparrows
in Brazil, or Haiti, or Harlem,
or the ones in south-central LA?

Sparrows shot down
or starved, or ill, or frozen--
    falling before their time,
but old alone sparrows too.
Then where is the God of the Sparrow,
    and is marking enough?

Oh, Father God, we sparrows
    are falling, falling, falling ...
we litter your holy ground.

ACCOUNTABLE

&

He stands in the pulpit
on Sunday mornings
in his black robe
    and tells us
we are accountable
      for the starving children
        in Ethiopia
      and the desperate boatloads
        sent back to Haiti
and for the five million
    homeless children
      in Brazil
and for our homeless here,
      sleeping under the viaduct.
He says it in the pulpit
    and in Bible study classes
    and in casual conversation:

we are accountable.

VISIT TO OUR SON

Drab
  bare
    dusty
sandy
  dry
    brown
      spare
it seemed to us.

But to him,
each mesquite tree,
  ironwood tree,
    creosote bush,
each jojoba,
  or cactus,
though thorny,
is beautiful.
Each one has meaning
  to him
and so to us.

The patch of green grass
in his back yard,
the palm tree
with its tiny green dates,
   the loaded grapefruit tree,
    the ramada
he built himself,
and the hammock he hung
  for us to lie in
are more than sufficient.

It seems to us
a far-off place--
  and strange--
but wonderful
  in the entire and
basic meaning
  of that word.

LAKE DISTRICT, ENGLAND

Take it all--

    all the green beauty of it
      all the clear rushing water
        and the dry-stone fences
    climbing up and over and across
              the steep fell-sides

        the gray horned sheep
        black lambs
          scarving mists
            fine quiet rain
       the lush greenness--

take it all
    and tuck it into a secret place
to tell over and over
    in a time
      when you have need

of beauty.

ECHO LAKE

Down to the water's edge
   the trees stand, dark-massed, forbidding.
The lake, mysterious, cold, and deep,
   molds to the land as if fitted
by its careful glacier maker.
   I hesitate to spoil perfection,
then hold my breath and take
   the cold and purifying plunge.
Baptized, I turn and lie in water,
   surrender to water,
   lie cradled in water.
Suspended under the sky,
   held in the cupped hand of the shore,
I drift, moved only by the motion
   of the water--almost bodiless,
lightly breathing, totally trusting,
   wombed in water,
         accepted as I am.

MAES HOWE

&

In chattering groups
  we follow the worn path
toward the ancient mound
  grass-covered and blunt
against the pewter sky.
  Stooping, stooping low,
one by one in semi-darkness
  we enter the long rock passageway,
emerging awe-struck
  into the great domed chamber
where runes remember
  the long-ago builders
stacking stone upon stone
  to seal their honored dead
in a strange land forever.

We mark their careful work
  and know their stoic hearts
high-vaulted as the chamber.
  Silently we finger-trace
the seal, the serpent,
  and the dragon carvings,
the runic messages they left
  to man or god,
overlaid but not obliterated
  by grafitti scratched
into the stones
  by Viking pillagers,
who came not to build
  but to destroy.

Crouching low reluctantly to exit,
    in single file along the narrow corridor,
we are born into the grey-bright day
    of our world, different now.

And know our deepest longing
    to build for our own eternity
        a giant mound against the one-ever sky.

BLOOD MEMORIES

Surely there is in us
--even now--
blood memories
of swelling seas
and high-prowed ships
glinting battle-axes
and victory bonfires.
Surely even now
there linger in us
green islands
mountains buttressed
scarving mists
fat spotted cattle
black-faced sheep
antlered stags
fish leaping
grain yellowing.

Surely there still keep
　　　the smell of the sea
　　　in our nostrils
the dawn in our far-away eyes,
and quiet, sweet rain on our eyelids
　　　the sun in one hand
　　and the moon in the other.
Surely there is yet
　　　seeded in the blood
　　　the keening cry
　　　　the triumphant yell
　　　the harp's song.
Then there must be celebration
　　　of where we have been,
　　　threading hope
　　　to where we are going--
blood memories of heroes
　　and great impossible deeds
　　curving back to find us.

TO LIVE

To live within sight and sound
  of the sea
and within the clasp
  of the mountains...

To have the silver-riffled lochs
  and the roiled and banked clouds
behind the mountained islands...

To drink in silvered sun-puddles
  on a single patch of sea--
      black-faced horned sheep
        on heathered hillsides
      splashing peaty burns
        and heavy-shouldered peaks--
    mist-scarved, mysterious--
      green and yellow fields,
        rolled hay and grain stooks
      sleek fat cattle
        stacked-rock fences
      and silvered, shadowed light...

To dwell here in this place
    would be to live
      as a merest mortal camped
    at infinity's gate,
      each day a tender verse
    of a poem without an ending
      and the knowing a special grace.

COVENANT

&

This--
this is holy ground,
   God-created,
   God-lavished:
this sweet April land--
   this sturdy green,
these dandelions and violets,
   these anemones and bluets,
the honking geese overhead,
   the clear, fast-running stream,
the green-tipped ridges--all.

   Kneel then,
kneel on this holy ground,
   bury your face in the riotous grass,
clutch it in your hands;
   breathe it in.
Turn over and look up
   through apple blossoms
at God's wide sky.
   Be filled up
again and again
   with all the wonder;
laugh out loud
   in the joy of it--
this living, loving,
   growing covenant--
partners in the grace of it.

Smell the God-scent
   on your hands.

IONA

Iona, blessed island,
   wave-washed, wind-scoured,
   rain-nurtured, sun-lightened,
we come to your rocky shores,
tentative pilgrims,
bearing our baggage.

   You are a real island,
   not a white Avalon,
   with sheep and cows
   and fisher-folk
   and craft shops
   and ruins.

Along the steep and narrow path
we find the somber, ravaged walls
of the nunnery, once home to Benedictines,
then McLean's west-weathered cross--
and farther on, St. Oran's chapel
with the graveyard, resting place
for kings, holy men, and commoners.
And then, here are the crosses
standing stark against the sky--
St. Martin's and St. John's--
and here, the ancient, massive abbey.

   To this place came Columba,
   fugitive and exile,
   searching for refuge
   out of Ireland's sight--
   a holy man in a coracle

afloat in treacherous waters,
    bringing with him his Christ.
Here we come, centuries later,
in the dark and drenching rain,
to the quiet, God-filled Abbey
overlooking the ever-changing sea,
seeking the blessing of its peace.

We come to the Abbey at night
 to sing old hymns--
all of us come from across the seas,
from the whole world over,
a hundred or more gathered together,
but small and vulnerable
in the great bare vaulted chamber
to hear the Word in this sanctuary.
We partake of His Body and Blood
with candle-glow on our faces,
passing the loaf along,
breaking off our bit of bread,
then sipping each from the chalice,
like handing a lighted candle
carefully down the generations,
sheltering the flame
and keeping it alive--
to give, in sacred trust,
to those coming next in line.

    Full-hearted, filled up,
    cradled in the continuity
    and the sweet-scented hush,
    we know, heart-pierced,
    the reaching back
      to the moments
    of Creation
      and the Cross.

Caught close--and hand-in-hand--
in the "do-this-in-remembrance-of me,"
we find in the here and now
the Resurrection
and the Life.

Outside is St. Columba's moon,
unexpected after the rain--
moonshine trailing on the sea,
and the dark crosses silhouetted
against the bright sky
and the silence
within and without--
full August moon shining
over his Abbey in this holy place--
shining too, this same moon,
over the place we came from
and to which we must return.

Iona of the crashing waves
and the bare rock pinnacles
and white sheep on green grass
and white doves flying
Iona of the ancient crosses
and the great revered abbey
Iona now of quiet memory
and linkage and exultation,
we leave you much lighter
than we came.

CERTAINTY

He is certain
that doubting is sinful,
sees no need, no room
    for doubts,
and certainly not
    for argument.
Every time there is
    a question,
he slaps his hand
on his leather-covered
zippered Bible
    and declares,
"These are the very words
    of God."
He likewise sees
no need for, no credibility
    in scholarship
    or archeology.
It is all right there,
    zippered tight and
    inviolate, inerrant.
God guided the hands
    who transcribed it;
they were His amanuenses.
    Secure in his passionate,
gleeful wrongheadedness,
he entertains no doubts.

Sometimes, in my frustration,
 I even envy his
       inerrant certainty.
I am, no doubt, a sinner.

PERSPECTIVE

PERSPECTIVE

&

After his wife shouted
    that company is here,
old Obie did his part:
    he cleared the front porch,
by kicking each hound dog off
    with well-placed dusty boots.
Now the old man sits relaxed
    in his rump-sprung chair
rocking and chewing.
    Occasionally he spits.
  We talk, he rocks.
Have you traveled much? I ask.
    Oh, some, he says. 'Nuff.
Ever get out of the county?
    Yessir.
Out of the state?
    Nawsir. Never wanted to.
 Not even to see what goes on
in other places? I persist.
    Nawsir.
Ever been to Lexington, then?
    Once't, he says.
And…how did you like that?
    Well, he says, rocking, chewing--
        speculative, then certain,
        he spits, then says:
    Hit won't 'mount to nothin'--
        Hit's too fur away.

ABIDE

Abide, abide, she crooned,
rocking the cradle
while the baby screamed.

I can't abide a dirty face –
moistening a corner
of her apron with her spit
and scrubbing at a cheek.

Love will abide, you'll see,
as the train pulled away
and she was smaller and smaller
on the platform.

Abide with me, she sang,
white-haired in her pew
and tears standing in her eyes,
fast falls the eventide,
the darkness deepens. . .

Lifting her chin, looking beyond,
as she held his hand –
God and the hills abide,
as we do, she said,
. . . abide.

ADVICE

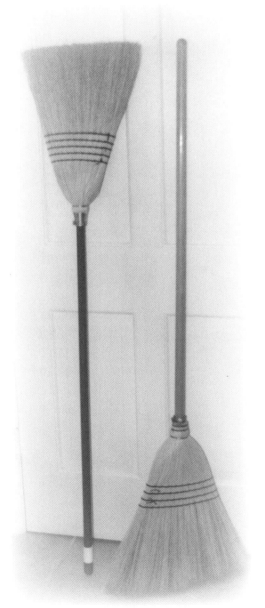

My mother always says,
grasping the broom
   to set it firmly
upside down
   on the handle-end,
"Never, never put
   your broom away
bristles down, or
   you're certain to marry
yourself a poor man."
   She married a poor man
and lived and loved with him
   nearly fifty years,
until he died.
   Yet she eagerly passes on
this bit of unassailable advice
   to all who, luckless,
turn our bristles down.

CONFLICTING ADVICE

&

She of the stern
    uncompromising eyes--
my mother,
    always restless,
would constantly
    admonish me:
Come, get a move on,
        please--
give it a lick
    and a promise
and finish up.
        Hurry!

And he of the twinkling
    knowing eyes--
my father,
    hoping to help me
to cultivate
    patience
and pride
    in a careful job,
said simply,
    make haste
        slowly.

ARCHEOLOGIST

Sometimes I am an archeologist
   digging patiently and carefully
through layered, hard-packed years,
   hoping to find artifacts
and majestic ruins
   of my former selves.
Other times I wield the shovel
   to bury them even deeper,
for no self of mine seems worthy
      of all the dusty labor
      of total excavation.

CHOOSING SIDES

"What side are you on?"
   I asked.
"Well, now, I don't rightly know,"
   he said.
"There's inside and outside
upside and downside,
front side and backside,
my side and your side,
our side and their side,
his side and her side,
winner's side and loser's side…"
   I sighed.
"Seems to me that sometimes
there's only one side,
and other times there's more sides
than a dog has fleas.
I reckon choosing sides
   Is tricky business
And calls for careful consideration."

MATZOS

Each year during Lent
I buy a box of Passover matzos--
   crisp thin squares of unleavened bread--
in remembrance of my father, a Jew.
   A Reformed Jew who never
went to synagogue
   but led a Christ-like life.
Back then I ate matzos with him
   protesting that they tasted
like corrugated cardboard, toasted.
   "Eat, Chick," he said, "and think
about your roots; it is soul food
   for whatever your religion.
You are missing something good."
   He was trying to sound like
     a real Jew.
Twinkling eyes betrayed him.

He's a long time gone now,
   and I live my life
in the shadow of the cross.
   No sacrificial blood
marks my doorposts,
   but sadness enters my home,
     and lingers.
   For him and happy memories
I eat my matzos now--
   but smeared with butter
     and sprinkled with sugar--
to compensate, most probably,
     for saltlessness.

PET NAME

&

I am sixteen,
   driving for four years,
so I should know better.
   It is Saturday.
I go in the side door
   of the garage
and back the car out--
   back it out
without opening the big door.
   Which splits in two--
heart-cracking--
   and glass shards tinkle, tinkle
      to the concrete.
Mother stands on the back porch,
   hands on hips, grimacing, angry.

My Dad comes out to see--
   says only, "Pull the car up, Chick."

I once asked my father, a Reformed Jew,
   if he believed Jesus was the Son of God.
"No," he said, "I think
   he was the best *man* who ever lived."
So, I decided, if Dad goes to Hell,
   I plan to be right there with him.

Fifty-five years later,
   thinking back to
      the garage-door day--
I just now have realized:
   (for whatever it's worth)
my mother never had
            a pet name for me.

RECOLLECT WHAT ALICE SAY

I ran to her that time
   with my white hurt
and my frustration
   (not yet understanding anger).
She wiped my tears
   on her flat worn-gingham bosom,
clasped me tight in her black arms.
   Your heart will heal, she said,
and I knows you will forget
   this hurt and others, child,
but I wants you to recollect
   forever what Alice say to you now:
         never, never, never
         let the sun go down
         on your wrath.

PRETTY IS

ॐ

Pretty is as pretty does,
   she says, wiping away
tears and blackberry juice
   with the hem
of her flour-sack apron.
   Your arms is scratched
and your braids's ravelin'
   and your socks is
fulla stick-tights.
   It'll take a month of Sundays
to pick 'em off.
   You's almost a grown young lady,
and I'se about give up on you.
   You insists on ridin' bareback,
you stays up in trees
   readin' your books
or hangin' upside down
   and you ain't learned
the first thing 'bout
   keeping your knees together.
I done ironed your pink dotted-swiss
   ten times over
hopen' to see you in it.
   You might as well be snakes-n-snails
and puppy-dog tails.

No, never you mind,
   when your teeth comes in good
and you fills out a mite,
   you'll turn out right pretty,
and whilst you're waitin
   you might go wash your face
and comb your hair
   and smile with your lips shut.

Pretty is as pretty does,
   I always says.

FINALITY

There is something so
   intimately final
about brown leaves
   covering the ground--
brown, dead leaves,
   individually and collectively,
like wasted minutes,
   defying both the deed
   and the imagination
to reverse the process--
   recover the loss.

PREDICTION

Late summer's amber moon
   hangs low over the mountain.
The mountain looks like forever.
   The same moon over the same mountain
has been watched by other eyes,
   but I think of the summer's passages
as I listen to the cello voices
   of cicadas foretelling frost
and the miniature roar of the brook
   chasing itself down the rocky slope.
Knowing August moon will turn to
   harvest moon and winter moon,
I stand here to watch tonight's moon
   climb higher, turn paler and colder.
I see no stars on this bright night.

The same moon I will see
   on other summer nights
from different places,

   but I will be different then.

ABANDONING

ॐ

On this day of chilly wind,
fast-scudding clouds,
    and fickle sun,
when pain finds
    all the interstices,
I look for distraction
    outside, around the cabin.
So I wonder that all the daffodils
    and narcissus are facing south,
and that only the tiny, delicate bluets
    open their four wee petals to the sky.
I see that honey bees are out working
    the purple spires of wild hyacinth,
and that a solitary plum tree blooms
    in the still-quiescent orchard.
    With my pup warm in the lea of my back
I lie in the cool new grass
    eye-level with hyacinths and bees,
smelling fresh-sawn cedar
    and hoping for the sun.
I dream, then, of once-brown hair
    and strong lithe legs
and running down the orchard hill
    in joyous abandonment,
with the wind blowing in my face
    and the children, laughing, at my heels.
    Only then I know I must not abandon
myself to pain--but rather to dreaming--
    and memories of youth and health and joy,
and hours to come
            of sun and rain
    and wind and flowers
        and all the rest
            of our long and lovely love.

RIPENESS

Proud
  plump
persimmons
  hang heavy
and hard
  on a slender tree--
untasted, inviolate.

Only after penetrating frost
  has stripped off
the leaves
  and humbled
the fruit
  are they soft
and sweet
  to eat.

VARMINT DOG

Yah, that's a blue-tick--
coon dog, naw...
    she's jest a varmint-dog.
Coon could lay down next her--
    she's a varmint-dog all right.
She likes ground-hogs--all sizes.
    Paid six hunderd for her--
wife near throwed me out.
    Well, won't no ground-hogs
get my garden this year,
        I reckon sure.
Won't get past this-here varmint-dog.
    She's right good at what she does.

STALEMATE

Billy clears away everything
in the path of his fences,
totally single-minded.
   Today we stand, silent,
facing each other,
   he kicking at dry mud clods
as he mulls over
   my edict
that he leave untouched
   the hollow fencepost
where the bluebirds
   nest each year.
His sweaty brown chest
   and belly quiver
with indignation.
      I have offended
                  his straight-line
         sensibilities.

HIGHWAY TEN TWENTY-EIGHT

Along the sides
  of county highway
ten twenty-eight,
    heavy-headed fescue ripples,
      thigh-high,
and purple spiky thistles
    are white with gravel-dust.
Wild roses bloom, lavish--
    pink and white--
in slides of plastic jugs,
    refrigerators, wading pools,
and wringer washing machines.

Mobile homes perch
    on narrow slate-heap ledges,
and the blue-light TV is always on.
    Jeans fill the lines
in rain and sun,
    while ragged couches and swivel rockers
moulder on the porches.
    Old lilac and snowball bushes
persevere in yards
    of empty-windowed houses,
and in wet-weather creek beds
    cat-tail-red Ford pick-ups
rust alongside
    ancient wheel-less Buicks.

But on the road's-edge knobs--
    in the little graveyards--
the dead lie,
    mowed and tended,
and their plastic flowers
      only slowly fade.

SHEEP

On a cold winter
   Sunday afternoon,
we found old Annie
   muttering and railing
about the morning's sermon.
   "Somebody has got
to get to that man--
   that city boy,"
   she said,
"Afore he makes
   a sartin fool
outa hisself.
   He can't even
read the Scriptures right.
   He talks on and on
about he has got
   to lead his sheep.
And I asks you
   just two things:

                    don't he know
                       we ain't his sheep,
                    and least-ways,
                    don't he know nothing
                 at all--any fool
                    has any 'quaintance
              with sheep can tell him--
                 purely, without a doubt,
                    sheep has got
                       to be *drove*."

THE MARTHA

Oftentimes I think
that I am hard of understanding.
    I hear the Word from the pulpit
and I think, "Yes, Lord, I hear you
    but I don't know as how
I've got this worked out just right."
    There is some of the stories
that I study and study on
    but I just can't get the sense of.
Now Mary and Martha--
    I know that Mary come out
looking like she cared the most,
    hanging on every word He said.
But I see Martha's part regardless--
    someone has got to see to things,
and it wouldn't hurt Mary one whit
    to get up and put the coffee on.
As I say, I hope the Lord
    keeps patience with me.
Another is the one about the father
    who went out and killed the fatted calf
for that trifling boy who went off --
    went clean off to another country
and left his father with all the chores.
    Didn't turn hisself to home
until he had most nearly starved to death.
    And he gets welcomed like he was
a hero just for coming back--
    and the good and faithful son
who stayed on at home to help out
    and labored mightily in the vineyard

got his nose all out of joint
     when his father killed the fatted calf
when he never even had a goat-kid
     for hisself and his friends.
No sir, not nothing for being faithful--
     not a ring, not a fine robe--nothing--
and chastised for being put out, too.

     I reckon my glass I'm looking through
is smudged dark as a dirty lamp chimney,
     because I feel real close to that elder son,
the good one--and Martha too.
     I might admire to be like Mary,
but I think most likely
     I'd put the pot to boiling.
I know I would.

THE VIEW

I know you was expectin' me,
Lord, and here I am,
   after another visitation.
I knowed they'd drive out
   today from the city,
as this is the first warm pretty spell
   we've had since back in December,
and they can't wait no longer
   for spring, to smell the good air.
I redded up the house
   and washed and did up my hair
so they wouldn't catch me
   looking like who-shot-Lizzie.
Baked a blackberry cobbler
   and put the coffee on
and tried not to act surprised.
   But they was all hot today
     and full of words
     and righteous wrath.
They made out like I let it happen.
   Rape of the mountains, they said,
pillage and plunder and desecration.
   Obscene they said, over and over,
     until my ears was ringin'.
Like I had just set here and
   called in them trucks and dozers
and put them to work on Furnace.
   Now I been watchin' for months, Lord,
and them machines look to me
   like puny ants busyin' theirselves
back and forth and round and round

on top of a giant-size anthill
a'carryin' off the carcasses
   and the leavins.
I've lived in sight of Furnace Mountain,
   as you know, all my life long,
      and I am near about
      as old as them hills,
and I can't say my heart and eyes
      ain't been grieved.
But I mislike my kin and
   them they've married up to,
comin' in here and allowin'
   as how I let them dozers in--
give them rights and all--
   just to punish *them*.
When their mouths is stopped with cobbler,
   I opens mine and says to them,
      as calm as I can muster,
I can see one thing right clear--
   clear as I see that bald dusty mountain there:
      you folks has clean forgot
         what it is like
         to be *pore*.

I expect I wasn't speakin'
   out of Christian charity, Lord,
but what was stickin' in their craw,
   and they was layin' to my account,
was the spoilin' *of the view.*

TWO OWLS

&

Two small owls
   in their sober grey-brown Sunday suits
came to visit on my window sill--
   it was a chilly, pewter morning--
twins, they seemed, identical
   in their gleaming golden stare.
Transfixed, I crept closer
   until only the window
      was between us.
Unblinking, they regarded me,
      a silent inquisition
unlike my own awed curiosity,
      and I, unnerved
at their penetrating scrutiny,
      tried simply to admire
their immaculate feathered finery--
   but failed, so I blinked first.
Occasionally a head would swivel,
   perhaps to reconnoiter my habitat.

   Almost mesmerized,
our unhurried gazes interlocked,
      I began to wonder
         how I could ever measure up,
         what standing
      I would have in their regard.

Eventually one flapped away;
   the second followed leisurely,
     leaving me alone--
       somehow bereft, exposed.
And as I slid the window open
    I was sure I could hear
     their comments
about the strange creature
    they had encountered,
examined, evaluated, assessed,
    and maybe identified.

I imagined what
    and to whom was their report.

And I was almost brought to tears.

EDEN

&

It all goes back to Eden,
   I suppose.
Surely man in total evolution
   cannot be to blame
for war and revolution,
   for unfed, unwashed millions
who herd together
   seeking food and solace.
Man, left to his own devices,
   could not have dreamed of
children maimed and dying,
   lands despoiled and wasted,
seas and air polluted.
   Man, with his dreams
could not have spun out
   the subtle aberrations:
the cheating and the lying,
   the shifting feet of justice,
the daily little murders…
   All, all go back to Eden.

Man, poor man,
   never could conceive
the helplessness of age,
   frustration and despair,

and fruitless searching
   after pattern and design.
It must go back to Eden.
   How else explain
man's enmity for man,
   his yearning to be free,
his lust for wealth and power,
   the warping of his soul?
Man, by himself,
   could not invent
the petty thefts,
   deceit from friend to friend,
the mocking Absolute,
   the yawning deaths.
But who to blame?

Perhaps those first progenitors.
   Or, better still,
the environment,
   too permissive,
too sensual, too tempting,
   yes, the environment,
there in the early Garden.

SHAKER SKETCHES – PLEASANT HILL 1980

&

1

Late in February
a golden willow
appliqued
   against a stark black
Shaker barn
   eloquently speaks
      of spring.

2

Through wavy-glass panes
   set in two-foot walls
I see stacked-rock fences
   corral unruly hills,
while tranquil thoughts
   sketch charcoal trees
on pale pewter skies.
   Nothing changes
      after all.

3

Prim tall commodious houses
   with sharp edges
and stoic windows
   saw orderly celibate lives
come and go
   through separate doorways
up separate stairs
   tie brooms and dip candles
sort seed, work looms--
   Artifacts remain.

4

Patrician spiral stairs
   curl upward
inside rectangular houses
where chairs hang tidily

from pegs on walls.
Virginal white and sober grey
and right angles
everywhere recount
sturdy, forthright craftsmen.
   --Unexpected,
like the sweet curve
of a young breast
under prim starched cotton,
like a love lyric
straying in and out
of a prayerful mind,
the long, lovely curves
wind up and up--
   grace notes for utility.
            5
There were no walls
  to separate
the men's side
  from the women's--
only wide hallways.
  Did no one stray across
or slip shadow kisses,
  clasp hands
on dusky paths,
  trade candle-glow glances?
No turbulent passions
  beneath blinder-bonnets
and round black hats?
  Did unfertilized dreams
and aching empty wombs
 hasten
        their
                demise?

Nothing
      changes
            after all.

SHAKER DREAM

Shakers led their separate lives
   together, sisters and brothers--
sworn celibates--
   adopted orphans
and hoped for converts
   to fill their communal houses.
With an eye to the future
   they built cradles
and highchairs
   and, with expectant love,
sowed their crops,
   gathered their harvests,
and sold their seed
   to the outside world.
As their numbers dwindled
   they said they gave
their hands to work
   and their hearts to the Lord.
Their bodies they traded
      for a dream.

GATHERING

&

On this windy day
   at winter's edge
I gather sticks
   in Sourwood Hollow--
sticks and branches
   the wind has brought down.
I bend and straighten,
   filling my arms
and making great jumbled heaps.

   And I think of you, my sisters,
the world over--
   in Ethiopia, in Pakistan,
in Somalia, Haiti, Cambodia--
   women now alive and women gone--
stretching back before memory--
   all of us bending and gathering.
But I know I gather to tidy up,
   and you gather desperately
for fuel--for warmth, for food.
   Oh, my sisters, I see you
wherever you are, bending
   and gathering your faggots,
scratching for warmth,
   competing for sustenance.
And I am here
   in my still-green valley
with my woods full
   of fallen branches and trees.
I call you here, my sisters,
   to gather with me.

We are in close company
    this windy day,
and I would share
    more than compassion with you.
I would place my bundle
    on your meager fire
to make the flames burn hot,
    or draw you here
for a great in-gathering
    to sit with me and all of us
at my abundant hearthside.
    Oh, we must gather together, sisters,
that we all may be warm and fed!

Now, with full arms and full heart,
    I am here alone in Sourwood Hollow,
watching smoke from the cabin chimney
curl upward to our one sky--
        knowing my plenty,
        feeling your want.

LOST INNOCENCE

&

The phoebe's frantic cries
pierced my early morning's dreaming.
    Back and forth through the open dogtrot,
screaming her anguish, wings beating,
    she passed her nest again and again,
lighting at last on the old rocker's arm.

    Each year she had returned to build
her nest of moss and mud on the narrow rim
    of the doorframe of the opposite cabin room--
fragile, protected, precariously perched.
    Expectantly we waited for her each spring,
then watched guarded creamy eggs transmute
    to clustered nestlings' open yellow beaks--
to feathered fledglings' shaky flights.

    She flew to the overhanging maple's branches
when I came out to check the nest;
    it overflowed with fledgling birds,
motionless and unblinking when I reached up to touch.
    The phoebe darted past as I stood on a stool
to lift them out--immobile work of nature's art,
    molded together as one piece, nest-shaped--
all perfectly formed and feathered--
    and dead--all dead--no mark upon them.
I held them in cupped and disbelieving hands--
    while mother phoebe braked and wheeled and cried.

    What monstrous thing had come by night
to rob them of their breath and life
    and steal away their warmth?

How explain the terrible catastrophe befalling
    these innocents in their sanctuary--
what evil had the mother done,
    her babies sacrificed to what avenging god?

    I buried them and grieved--
        no explanation coming,
        no mystery unsealed.

    That phoebe never came again
to make her nest above the cabin door.
    The nest she left behind
shattered and fell apart,
    leaving only mud-stain on the logs
in remembrance of the inexplicable--
    no answer to my bafflement,
no balm to her bereavement.
    And I, mere mortal, unappeased--
somehow lost an innocence
    I didn't know I had.

VIETNAM WAR MEMORIAL

We are drawn, slowly,
this sultry summer almost-dusk,
   into the dark embrace
of those bright-polished
   tapering black-granite wings.
Then we are in the presence--
   we, nameless now--
of those names,
   gray-etched
into the somber granite,
   names converging at the apex--
      1975 meeting 1959.
And in the moist rice-paddy heat
   a woman hangs over the top
making a pencil rubbing
      of a name.
"Get the one on either side,"
   a man directs her.

A tall immaculate man
   in a blue-gray suit,
with a blue handkerchief
   in his breast pocket
turns off the last notes
   of the Mendelsohn tape
      he was playing
and his wife stands by
   with the video camera
on her shoulder
   pointed at him
as he glues the service ribbons

beside the name
and sticks the carnation cross
   in the crack
at the foot of the wall.
   He is red-faced, grimacing
with the effort of not crying.
   His blonde teen-aged son,
in long flowered shorts
     steps aside
and darts a quick glance.
   "Twenty years,"
he says to everyone and no one.
   "Twenty years today."
Tears collect in his eyes
as they move off together,
   anonymous now too
in the press of quiet people.

Name by name by name
     by name,
we are with a host
   clasped by great black wings
amid a silent beating clamor,
   seeing ourselves in
the shining surface,
   being given back
ourselves
   in bloody pieces
by the gray
     etched names.

FIRE-SETTING

$\text{\reflectbox{S}}$

There's a trick
  to starting a fire
and having it do
  what you want--
no less and no more.
  Part depends, of course,
on what you have
  to work with:
tinder, matches, kindling,
  flint and steel, paper,
minds, trash, twigs,
  logs, souls, brush--
    whatever--
(highly combustible or
  slow to ignite).
And success with fire
  involves what you expect
from it: heat, light,
  cooked food, fear,
cleared undergrowth,
  revolution, insights--
any or all of the above.

There's a knack
to lighting a fire,
  getting it going,
feeding the flames--
  a skill to using
its light and its heat
  and its power,
without letting it burn

out of control,
singeing--or even destroying--
the fire setter.
There's a risk,
and sometimes a glory,
in setting a fire--
in letting it become
a force of its own.

PHOTOGRAPH: IRANIAN SOLDIER

On the glossy page, in color:

he lies in youthful grace,
    cushioned almost tenderly
on a bed of tiny yellow desert-flowers--
    lies on his side,
legs apart as if for comfort,
    hands folded together under his cheek
      as if in peaceful sleep.
He has no shoes on,
    as if he pulled them off
      before he lay down,
and his trousers are tucked
    neatly into his socks.
Grey desert dust powders him over,
    and the flowers are dusty too,
so that he and the scene
    are a faded still-life,
      like a chiaroscuro.
He seems relaxed, resting,
    and no blood shows.
His mother is not there
    to pull the covers up
or to tuck the curl behind his ear
    before the ponderous rumble
      and the Iraqi tank comes
      to press him and the flowers
      down into the desert dust.

Turn the page.
Go on to news of other wars.

RUN NAKED

&

Should I strip and run naked,
    shouting, "Look at me--
I have pared down
    to the essentials--
this is what I really am--
    look at me!"
Then how would my neighbors
    greet me?
Would they clasp nakedness
    to their bosoms,
welcoming the essential me,
    glad to be confronted
by the genuine article,
    stripped of artifice?
Or would they turn away
    in horror and disgust?
And would they turn and flee,
    preferring me in clothing,
        or not at all?

SKEPTICAL

Why is it
   that I become
most skeptical
   when I am surrounded
by a proliferation
   of wisdom?
Why is it
   that what I most long
to hear
   is somehow
         inaudible?
And why
   do I yearn
most deeply
   to be
what I will never be?
   Why?

THE CATECHISM

Oh, my sweetling, oh, my wee one,
so snug in your unknowing,
whatever will befall you
in the long years that lie ahead--
who will you someday be?

My energetic little one,
ceaseless in your exploring,
what do you want to be
when you get to be much bigger?
    I want to be this high, like Daddy,
    and take a big briefcase to work.
    Learn to read.

What do you want to be
when you grow up, my son,
changing even as I watch?
    I want to be a fireman, Dad,
    a scientist, or an astronaut.
     Maybe a magician.

What now are you thinking, son,
that you will like to be
when you are grown?
    I want to be successful--rich,
    have a fast car and a good woman.
    Climb Everest.

Now that you are almost a man,
what do you dream of being?
And what would you like to do?

I want to be a doctor now
and do just what you do.
Except not work so hard.

I see you deep in your profession, son,
and heavy with responsibility--
are you glad of what you are?
    I cannot think of anything just now
    that I would rather do or be.
    But life asks so much of me.

You have made your mark, my son:
your wife and children are doing well.
Is there anything else you wish you'd done?
    Taken time to play, I guess,
    time to mountain-climb and love.
    Enjoyed my wife and children more.

Since years have flown, father,
and time is growing shorter,
what do you think of now?
    Where have they gone, the years,
    and how did I get to this?
    There is much I still want to do.

You are now, how shall we say--
past your prime and holding.
What do you see ahead?
    Waning of body and mind
    while I still feel young inside.
    I really need to run and play and love.

Now that you have grown old, grandfather,
what is it that you hope to do or be,
say, five years from now?
    At peace with who I am, my son,
    and what I've done--
    content, and yes, oh yes--alive!

LEAVING

&

He was
eighteen
   when he left
the bosom
   of his family
and went away
   to school.
Never again
   did he return
as family--
   thereafter
he visited
   as observer,
as guest,
   as stranger.

PARAPLEGIC, OR "FEED 'EM ROCKS"

And so I *ride* my chair,
   the young man
in the black tee shirt
   with white letters:
Feed 'em Rocks!
   explains, chin held high.
After my wife left,
   I took the arms off
so I'd not be squashed
   down into it.
This way *I ride it.*

His own rejection,
   unlike his dead legs,
blazes live and raw
   as a new wound.
Defiant now,
   he casts rejection
      first,
like stones,
   into the teeth
      of pity.

NEW YEAR

&

This is the new year's
first new moon--
   a crescent nick
in grey sky-skin
   that lets a modest
light shine through.
   I'd like to think
it's an omen,
   a glimpse of the great
unquenchable light
   that will burn
a quiet hole
   of hope--
an aperture
   for winter moonshine
         to silver-seed
   this black tired earth
         with peace,
                  with peace.

PORTRAITS FROM LIFE

PORTRAIT

&

Quiet she lived
  and, quiet, died.
Her children were
  little inconvenienced.
Six months before,
  she tidily gave away
almost all her things,
  except her books.
Eventually she ceased to eat
  and later still, to walk,
and kept her bed.
  There was not much to say.
When at last her breathing stopped,
  they said it was a blessing.
During the final visitation
  they laughed and chattered
in front of the closed coffin
  they covered with red roses
and baby's breath for remembrance.
  Grandsons she seldom saw
shouldered the casket,
  and no one minded the cloudy day.
In the family graveyard
  her footstone awaited her,
engraved with her name
  and birthdate.

They said she knew them
to the end.

THE SAYER

&

"Well, now, my opinion
ain't worth a hill o'beans--
   and it frost-bit!"
feisty old Grannie Cross
   would declare--
and then she'd give it.
   When asked if
such and such
   would come to pass,
she'd say to us,
   "Well, if the Lord
      be willin'
and the creek don't rise."
   Which covered
nearly everything.

HIGHER MATHEMATICS

⳥

The weekend farmer,
  thinking to make conversation
with his farmer neighbor,
  scuffs the toes of his new
Red-Wings in the dust
   and asks,
How many days does it take
  a cow to eat a bale of hay--
one of those big rolled bales
  you've got lined up over there
at the edge of the field?
   The other,
sitting on his tractor,
  cuts off the engine,
takes off his cap
  to scratch at his head.
Finally he ventures:
  Well, I put two out
 for thirty
   ever other day.

THE CITY SLICKER

He was a city slicker
who fell in love
   with a country girl
teaching school in Louisville.
   He followed her home
to Bourbon County
   to meet her family and
convince her of his love.
   She had two sisters--
they liked his easy charm
   and gentle manners--
and two overalled
   and mettlesome brothers
who laughed at his white shirts,
   his pleated-front trousers
and pointed-toe, polished shoes.
   (He would never tell them
he was a champion Charlestoner.)
   Under guise of brotherhood,
they invited him
   to ride old Nellie home
from their other farm
   in Nicholas County--bareback--
some twenty-three miles of country road.
   Now Nellie had a sharp backbone
that protruded and was unavoidable
   unless he sat far back on her rump,
which he tried to do.
   He ate his meals off the mantel-piece
for days afterward and endured
   their jeers and taunts.

He happened to be a good marksman,
    so when they sent him out
 to shoot the skunk lodged
    under the corn crib,
he killed it with one shot,
    but not before it got to him.
Before they'd let him back into the house,
    he had to bury his clothes
    and bathe in lye-soap
and rinse several times in vinegar.
    But they had to crawl under
and fish the polecat out
    before it ruined their corn.
They sent him out at the end
    of a hot work day
to unharness the mule team.
    When they went out, finally,
to see what was keeping him,
    they found him neatly
piling pieces of harness
    in the feed bin--
a great heap of harness--
    over a hundred pieces there--
buckles and straps.
    It took them the best part
of a week to reassemble them.
    He offered to help,
but they declined.

He never had felt that
        he was anybody's fool.

SMITH '49

&

She stares stolidly
   at me from the newsprint
pages of the alumni newsletter:
   heavy-jowled, mannish haircut,
thick dark-rimmed glasses,
   lips straight, eyes steady.
Under the picture is
      Smith '49

In my dusty yearbook
   on the still-glossy page
she stands with a sheaf
   of long-stemmed roses,
her slim shoulders bare
   and her long, light hair
curling gently onto her bosom.
   Her smile is perfect
for a home-coming queen,
   and her tiny waist is perfect
for her escort's hand.
   I remember how she mugged
for the earnest student photographer
   and pulled out a rose for him
and kissed him to tease
   her sweetheart.
I remember how he chased her
   to claim his own kiss
now that she was a celebrity.

The article tells me
   she is an assistant professor
of library and government documents
   librarian at a college
      I never heard of.

A MARRIAGE

She killed him,
neatly and efficiently,
with a bloodless repertoire
  of daily little murders
accomplished with determination
    and finesse
into the ego's soft underbelly
and the tender environs
of his loving heart
  (he loved her).
  Though bewildered,
he never traded hurt for hurt,
offering himself up
at last as sacrifice
    to her need.
It took her forty years
    to kill him,
and the million tiny wounds
were invisible
    to the eye,
so she was free
to nurse him as he died,
patiently, (as he had lived),
proclaiming her faithfulness
and devotion, and her loss,
    and he let her,
      for he loved her.

A CRAVING WOMAN

She always said she was
a craving woman,
and she was.
  When she was little,
she craved a starched white dress
with little red flowers on it
and a hat that
wasn't a poke bonnet
and shoes for everyday,
not just for Sunday,
and some play-pretties.
  Later she craved
a regular buggy--
not a broke-spring wagon
with a board seat--and
a pair of matched mules to pull it.
  Next she craved
a man to do her bidding
and a hewed-log cabin
with bleached-ash floors
and a wood door
and real windows.
  She craved younguns
who would grow up
to be preachers or landowners
or marry men of means.
  Then she craved
a black taffeta dress
with silk medallions
and a little train.

     At the very last
she said she craved
a cherrywood coffin
to be buried in.
     They thought this
would finish up her cravings,
but she said,
stroking the cherrywood
and looking far away,
"I allus craved a red silk petticoat
with a wide lace flounce--allus did."
     But then she always told us
she was a craving woman.

UNCLE EVERETT

Uncle Everett snugs
   into the faded platform rocker
like an old tortoise
   into its shell.
His box of Tampa Nuggets
   is on the chipped table
close at hand,
   and his jug is down
by the side of his chair.
   He keeps the thin remnant
of Mattie's blue-and-white
   coverlet across his lap
and his red Prince Albert
   tobacco tin in his hands.

He likes the young home-
health-care
   nurse who comes to check
on him each Friday.
   He leans out of the hollow
of the chairback a little
   and bares his bony, hairless
chest to her stethoscope.
   He coughs a little while she listens.
He stops gumming the unlit,
   two-thirds-consumed cigar
while she questions him.
   He likes the feel of her fingertips
on his knobby wrist.

You seem fit as a fiddle to me,
Uncle Everett--how do you think
   you feel this week?

He is glad again
   that she doesn't say
remarkable for a man
   of ninety-three.

He spits delicately
   into the Prince Albert can
and closes the lid,
   gathering himself
for his customary:

Can't complain, missy.
   Nawsir, can't rightly complain.
But let me tell you something--
   if I'dve knowed I was going
to live this long,
   I'dve sure took
better care of myself!

And she smiles every time.
   And pats his hand.

ADAM'S OFF-OX

❧

Yep, he's mine--
just about as peculiar
and contrary
as Adam's off-ox,
I reckon.
Sets around readin
and talkin with the women-folks,
big as he is--
more'n six foot now
and seventeen.
Says he wants to go off
to the University
stead of farmin and loggin.
Borries books wherever
he finds them.
Likes figuren more'n anything.
I've seed him
driven the tractor
and readin.
  Don't cross me none,
and he's too big to whup.
It's a puzzlement
what's to come of him.
  Adam's off-ox,
that's all he is.

OLD MAN SNOWDEN'S DEAD

Old man Snowden's dead
   just took him out, they did,
Don't you hear them dogs
   a'his a'howlin?
Stuck their heads
   outa them caves he dug
for them into the sides
   of the hill backa his house--
you know them little caves?
   Put straw down in each one,
so they'd be snug
   and outa the cold and wet.
Cool in summers, too,
   and they liked 'em fine.
They lays in 'em looking out
   like they owned his little place.
Now the old man's gone, and
   them hounds keeps a 'howlin.
Betty--that's his daughter'n-law--
   says they drive her mad.
She's gonna take them
   to her place, if she can.
No one knowed he was ailin--
   Old Snowden's looked porely
ever since I was a tad.
   Mean as they come, he was.
But he loved them dogs.
   Brokedown's he was,
he'd out on the hills at night
   just to set on a log
and listen to' em run.

Couldn't hardly walk,
but he still could hear,
    and he knowed each one--
knowed the voice they give
    and where they was, exactly.
He loved them ever one, he did.
    They started acting queerly
yesterday--outa they heads--
    howlin' and howlin'
until his boy Rodney, he come
    to see what trouble was.
Snowden, they says, was at the store
    on Friday buying dogfood
and new collars, stout leather,
    looking same as always.
Didn't say nothin to nobody.
    Betty said she didn't miss him.
He was right peculiar--
    liked to live to hisself.
Said hounds was better company
    than any folks he knowed.
Well, they found him settin there,
    just settin, dead and cold, and stiff
as wash froze on the lines--
    carried him out still settin--
too stiff to lay him out.
    Kinda fittin, I'd say:
too stiff to bend, alive.
    Had to tie 'em up, them dogs,
to get him outa there.
    Well, just thought I'd stop by
to tell the news: old man Snowden's
    gone and bought his.
Betty'll take them hounds,
    I reckon, if she can keep 'em
long enough to sell 'em.

Won't nobody want 'em, though.
Might just as well, I say,
    take 'em out and shoot 'em.
Old man Snowden's dead,
    and they won't run for nobody else,
you'll see, not no one.
    Don't that howlin give you the willies?
Like wolves, I'd say.
    But Snowden's gone
and they can't call him back.
    Well, I best be goin.'
Thought I'd spread the news.
    Reckon most folks a'ready knowed--
that is, if they could hear, they did.

    Listen, now--just listen.
Don't that git you?

JESSIE

Having unexpectedly made it through another winter,
   old Jessie sits in the dog-trot rocker,
sunning herself like an ancient lizard
   in the late February sun.
Wrapped in a raggedy bed-quilt,
   with her felt Sunday hat pulled down
over her ears, only her thin curved nose
   and dark eyes show.
She never thought to see another spring.

Now she sits and watches snow melting
   and the water running off the hillsides
in runnels and rivulets to join the creek
   on the other side of the cabin.
Then she hears the phoebes in the trees
   although she cannot see them,
and she glances up sharply to see
   if the old phoebe's nest is still there
above the cabin door and is relieved that
   it too has come through another winter.
She remembers all the springs the phoebes
   have laid their eggs and hatched their young
and how she had always watched to see
   when the young fledglings had flown again.
Now she dreams, too, of her own young
   who filled the cabin rooms and left,
who now have flown far
   and some are forever gone.
She sees the pines sway in the wind
   and feels the sun warm on her face.

The years slide by like wind on her cheeks
    and she hears her mother's voice singing:

> *The north wind doth blow*
> *and we shall have snow*
> *and what will the birdies*
> *do then, poor things?*
> *They'll hide in the barn*
> *and keep themselves warm*
> *by hiding their heads*
> *under their wings,*
>   *poor things.*

Jessie rocks and sings and thinks
  about arriving at another spring.
Birds know how to get through the winter,
    she thinks. I don't know if they hide in a barn,
but I know--I've watched how they face into the wind.
    They don't turn their tails and get their feathers
blown inside out and themselves blown away.
    They winter over just fine and come back
to the nest and line it with moss
    and lay their eggs and start over.

She listens to the water running
    and hears the phoebes' clear calls
and is content in the winter sun.

THE GROWER

At eighty-three
    she wages unrelenting war
on weeds and clods,
    potato bugs and beetles,
rabbits in her lettuce,
    birds in her strawberries.
She roots them out,
    scares them off,
tamps them down
    quite as relentlessly
as in an almost-forgotten life
    she planted and cultivated
reading, spelling, arithmetic.
    She had no time for art or music,
for backtalk or excuses;
    now she refuses

to give in to bugs or weeds.
    She tolerates hard-baked dirt
no better than impervious minds.

It seems she always
    had the knack
        for getting the most
            out of vegetables
and people.

THE INEVITABLE

When she turned ninety
  she decided it was time
to sit down and wait
   for the inevitable to befall her.
She would think long thoughts
  and remember and compose herself.
She figured she had lived long enough.
  But her hands in her lap were ugly to look at
and her back hurt when she didn't move around.
  And the phone kept ringing
and the dog needed to be fed.
  Then the beans needed picking…
and the raspberries…
  and the grass kept growing.
She tried to nap several times a day
  but people kept coming in her front door
and the dog had to go out
  and her great-grandsons wanted to be read to
and the newspapers kept piling up
  because she had no time to read them
(but refused to throw them out unread).
  One day she took time enough
to read the date on the latest one
  and discovered that
another year had rolled around.
  And the calendar on which she had recorded
quarts of strawberries picked
  and packages of limas frozen
clearly said it was July again.
  And there was a robin singing in the apple tree
outside her kitchen window.
  She knew it was singing,
although she could no longer hear it.
She could still remember birdsong.

TEETH

ॐ

"Where are your upper teeth, Mother,"
   I asked, speaking into her good ear,
as I watched her gum
   the meat off a chicken leg.
(Her deafness covered a multitude of quirks.)
   She swallowed, then felt around
         in her mouth.
"Dunno," she mumbled
and resumed her eating.
   A careful search of her room--
her denture case where
   her lowers resided in algae-water,
her dresser drawers, the dirt
   around her plants (where I once found them),
the pockets of her pants and housecoats,
   her dirty-clothes pile--yielded nothing
but wads of used napkins, pilfered candy,
   and long-gone, secreted bananas.
Questioning of kitchen help
   and attendants who dressed her
turned up little--a few stale cookie crumbs.
   By then, some of the staff had joined the mission.
I felt all around her in her wheelchair,
   under her, while Kim lifted her up,
and in her lap--no pockets that day--
   and checked the rooms she was known
to raid each day for their stash of sweets.
   And no one knew how long they had been missing.
They had last found her hearing aid
   stuffed deep in a melting mound of vanilla
and had called me to come try to salvage it.

Mother was unperturbed
      but a little curious about the goings-on.
After more than an hour of searching,
      I stopped at the nurses' desk and told them,
"I give up. But if you come across upper dentures
      with the two front teeth missing, please call me."
They shrugged and grimaced sympathetically--
      they were used to frantic searches.
"Oh," said an attendant who had been busy elsewhere,
      "So that's who they belong to!"
And she fetched them from the nurses' workroom,
      carefully stored in a plastic bag.
With gratitude and in triumph
      I finally carried them back to my mother.
"Look," I exclaimed, showing the gleaming denture.
      She turned up her nose, screwed up her mouth--
"What are those," she demanded, "What are those?"
      "Your upper teeth," I shouted.
"Well, I wouldn't have anything like that in my mouth,"
      she declared, in her loud deaf voice. "No, sir!"
Deflated, I went to wash them and
      to scrub out the denture box.
When I returned to her, clean container in hand,
      and a hot soapy washrag to clean her up,
she looked up at me and said in her most carrying tones,
      "Well, Barbara, if you need you some new teeth,
I'll give you the money to get you some."

HEROES

&

He was carrying their gear
into the log-cabin room
across the dog-trot,
where they would
stay a couple of nights--
our tall son-in-law, Matt,
our daughter, and two small grandsons,
who would live here if they could.
The screened door slammed behind him

Then we all heard his shout,
panicky and urgent: "Dad, Dad!"
And we all came running.
And found Matt, sleeping bags
still under both arms, white-faced,
and nose-to-nose with a beady-eyed bat
hanging upside down from a rafter.
"Dad!" he yelled, "a bat!"
(My husband is five-feet-six,
and Matt is six-feet-five.)

The short guy stepped past,
nudged the paralyzed big guy aside,
reached up with his leather glove,
and plucked the bat off--
rather like picking fruit--
and carried it outside.
No one said a word--
not even the wide-eyed boys.
I have heard that heroes
are born, not made.

THE HEY, YOU
℘

He was home for the first visit--
    home from college his freshman year--
sitting at the kitchen table,
    animatedly describing the trials
and tribulations and adventures
    of this first semester.
He talked about his roommate,
    who snored and ground his teeth,
the guys who smuggled girls into their rooms
    to spend the night,
the cafeteria food, the local hamburger joint.
            The girls.
    In a pause, I asked him,
What about your classes?
    Aw, Mom, they're fine.
Any that really turn you on? I persisted.
    Not really, he said, But they're O.K.

I've wanted to ask you, son, but didn't dare before--
    why did you decide to go to college when
you always told us you just weren't academically inclined."
    Well, he said, I guess I don't really know.
We didn't push you--or, I don't think we did.
    I almost held my breath.

No, he said, you didn't ...thinking, searching:
    Let's put it this way: I know for sure
I don't ever, never want to work for anyone else.
    And some day, when someone yells, *Hey, you!*
I don't want to be the one who says, *Who, me?*
    That's it, Mom: I want to be the Hey, You--
        and not, not ever the Who Me.

And I--I took motivation where I found it.

DAY AT THE BEACH

We were all agreeing
    that it had been a perfect day
at the beach along the Jersey shore
    Grandparents from Tennessee
had made this longed-for
    outing possible for me
with three young children.
    Mid-afternoon, Anne, our toddler,
was asleep on the beach towel
    under the umbrella, and
the boys were still wave-jumping
    as the wind picked up
and the tide was coming in .
    So I really wanted to quit while I was winning.
There was a long drive ahead,
    and the tide was coming in.
I walked to the water's edge
    (which was now not as far away),
and directed the little boys to wash the sand off--
    that we needed to head home.
And I turned and walked back to the umbrella,
    the younger boy, David, on my heels.
We started packing up our things,
    but, when I turned around to call,
our older boy, Mike, was nowhere to be
seen.
    I expected him to pop up, triumphant,
from a wave,
but I could not spot him anywhere.
    And the tide was coming in.
Other beach-goers were leaving too,
    but they heard our calling out--
Dad went one way and I another.

He walked along the water's edge;
I waded knee deep in the foaming water,
    half-expecting him to wash up
against my legs and come up grinning.
    I looked back to see my Dad
growing ever-smaller in the distance,
    and I noticed others were fanning out
calling and checking under beach houses.
    I kept walking and looking back,
with growing fear in the pit of my stomach.
    No child in sight--no child at all--
and he was only four--a smart and stocky four,
        but still a little guy.
Would he be washed ashore,
    or was he hiding under a beach house, maybe?
This was not typical of him, I thought.
    And the tide was coming in.
I walked and ran and looked and called;
    long out of sight
of my umbrella and all the others,
    finally, reluctantly, I turned,
hoping, hoping he would be there when I got back.
    He was not, but my Dad was there--
and clumps of men who had been looking too.
    It was more than an hour and a half
since he had last been seen.
    Though sick with dread, I had not cried as yet,
but tears began as I started at last
    to trudge up to the beach patrol office,
which had been alerted earlier
    about the missing little boy.
I needed to--I must-- call my husband
    back in the city to tell him the awful story
of our beautiful, tragic day at the beach:
    I had turned my back for only a minute or two.
My parents and the other searchers
    were grim-faced, scared, and feeling helpless.
I was terrified now and almost mourning.

And the beach had become much narrower.
The tide was almost in now, and the waves were rough.
    Though I couldn't bear to call my husband
with the incredible news, I needed to stay calm.
    Then, just as I finally reached him, my legs shaking,
before we had spoken, even as I tried to begin,
    I saw a police car drive up, its passenger door burst open,
        and there was Mike,
safe--coated with sand and badly sunburned all over,
    bathing suit drooping underneath his little belly--safe!
As I dropped the phone, he ran toward me, calling out,
    "If I could read, Mom, I wouldn't have gotten lost.
There were signs all along the beach.
    Now will you teach me? Will you?"
            as he ran up the steps into my open arms.
    No tear-tracks on his red and sandy cheeks.
The policeman said ,"Fifty-two blocks down the beach
    I found him. Fifty-two. He said that *you* were lost."

SON, NOW

Now that it has recurred,
your young life flashes in my memory
like slides, illuminated, thrown up
before me on a screen:
    Click: You, newly born, wheeled out
with other newborns, wrapped up like loaves of bread,
and stuffed into slots to deliver to the mothers,
but you are bright-eyed and straining to see
and to get on with this new world.
Everyone laughs because you look
so out-of-place with newborns.
    Click: You, crawling into the ocean head-on,
with the waves washing over you.
    Click: You out in the back yard
while I unpack our few belongings,
stuffing a tree-frog in your mouth.
One of his legs hangs out, madly kicking.
    Click: You, at six, sitting at the kitchen table
reading the newspaper: "Mommy, what is rape?"
You pronounce it rah-pay.
    Click: You, walking to school with one foot
in the gutter and one on the curb,
looking earnestly for treasures.
    Click: You, sitting sulky in the classroom
while the teacher tells me
she doesn't like your attitude.
    Click: You, wrestling with your brothers,
red-faced, shouting, unwilling to stop.
    Click: You, bear-hugging your sister, laughing,
until I have to make you turn her loose.
    Click: You, standing stiff and proud with your father,
in your faded, starched Boy Scout uniform
to receive your Eagle award.

Click: You at Junior Awards night,
going down to the front again and again.
    Click You, stocky, bull-strong,
catching a pass and running down the sidelines
as if nothing in the world could stop you.
    Click: You, abandoned with all your belongings
in a tiny dormitory room with a pointed Gothic window.
    Click: You, sweating in the heavy green doctoral robe
and velvet hood in the June sunshine, your hair
hanging down your forehead under your mortarboard.
    Click: You, in your hospital whites, stethoscope dangling,
rumpled, heavy-eyed, sluggish, hardly you.
    Click: You in a tuxedo in a marble church
with a huge gilt crucified Christ,
tense, unsmiling, determined, alien,
with your new bride on your arm.
    Click: You, getting off the plane,
dragging your left leg, your left arm
hanging dead and useless at your side.
    Click: You, playing Santa and handing round
the gifts that same Christmas,
trying hard to be yourself and more.
    Click: You, all right, but out of focus now.
You are confused, disoriented, weary, ill.
You sit with your empty face,
holding your newborn son with one arm,
not looking at him.
        Click. Click. Click. Click.

SISTER
&

You need to understand
she was neither a screamer
   nor a screecher,
   nor a tattle-tale.
And certainly not inferior
   to mere boys.

All during her childhood and youth,
   she tried very hard
to civilize her three brothers--
   two older and one younger.
She shamed them into giving up
   their burping contests
and running around in their jockey shorts
   when her girlfriends came over.
She erupted with anger
   as well as giggles
when her oldest brother
   stuffed her best friend,
(whom he had christened motormouth),
   into the garbage can
because she wouldn't shut up.

When they were all in high school
   she made an appointment at a studio
to have their picture taken
   for their parents' Christmas present.
She selected clothes for each,
   laid them out and refereed
their taking turns at showers.
   The resulting portrait
   was a testimony to her patience.

All of this might lead
    you to believe that they
were very amenable to requests
    their sister made
and perhaps even treated her special.
But one of her earliest memories
    belies that supposition.
When she was a tiny little girl
    she had to perch on the very front
of the toilet seat, feet dangling,
hanging on to the seat
    with both hands to keep from falling in.
Her brothers, usually waiting much too long
    to interrupt their outdoor games,
would dash in, frantic and clutching themselves,
    to use the bathroom
only to find it occupied, at least partially.
    They felt there was sufficient room for both
and therefore proceeded to take care
    of their urgent need.

Whereupon their sister screeched her outrage
    and let go to swat at them as best she could--
            but awkwardly,
so it was inevitable that she would lose
    her already precarious balance
and lurch backwards into the yellow stream.

    Each of her brothers protested
that no disrespect was intended,
    (and her back was to them),
that there was plenty of room,
    and they really weren't bothering her
            anyhow.

COMPACT AND ENERGETIC

Mom, she yelled, Mom--
   loud enough to make him stop,
but not loud enough
   to summon help--
Mom, he's bothering me again.

He was the fourth child, third son,
   and was born, his mother said,
an absent-minded professor
   and suffered relapses
from time to time.

It took two to get him out the door
   to go to school each morning
to where the bus driver waited
   at the foot of the driveway
(knowing he'd never make it
   to the corner).
His sister tried to help him
   by making lists of things
he had to do that day,
   but he would lose the list.

His grandfather said he would
   be good help
if only he could keep him
   away from reading material.
He was always reading
   and supplying everyone
with information, wanted and unwanted,
   about what he had been learning.

It made for interesting
   dinner-time conversations
even for his brothers.
   His father predicted he would grow up
to be a corrupt politician--
   he could talk his way out of anything.

He was always a little small,
   but his mother told him
he would be a big man some day--
   if only so much wasn't turned under--
his feet were plenty big.
   At school during class change
when the principal--a stern, large woman--
   put her arm across the line to stop it,
He ducked under and kept going.
   And when she called him back,
he said, There are a *few* advantages
            to being small.
It was said she actually laughed.
   Playing basketball with the taller boys,
 he got so he could fake, dribbling,
   and dart under their arms for a lay-up.

And when his sister--two grades ahead--
   had a paper assigned in school,
she would come home to find
   her bedroom awash in opened books
featuring the newest topic at hand.
   There's more, he told her eagerly,
lots more; I'll get them.
   Whereupon she stamped her foot
and said no more, no more--
   too much; I don't want all this.
She called, Mom, Mom,
   He's bothering me again!

Years later, after his PhD
   and many papers, many digs,
several time a marathoner,
   and after he had made
an impressive name for himself,
   and was totally comfortable
in his muscular, thick-chested body,
   the interviewer described
the archeologist in charge
   of this important dig as
compact and energetic.

His nephews teased him;
     he didn't care.

STORIES

GREEN PAINT

We were two little girls--
    four or five maybe--
on a hot, sultry August day
    in Macon, Georgia,
many, many short years ago.
    So we were stripped
to our pink rayon panties,
    bored with tea-parties
under the china-berry tree
    and splashing in the old tin tub.
And we just happened
    to find a can
of green paint
    in the garage
and managed,
    two little girls, now--
        to pry the top off.

Here, it gets a little vague,
    because I don't remember
our finding a paint brush,
    but somehow we painted
        each other green,
thoroughly green--
    bright green.
Except for our hair and eyes
    and what our panties covered--
        green.
(I think it was because
    we feared the repercussions
if we painted anything
    that mattered.)

My mother screamed
    when she found us--
screamed and cried,
    as a matter of fact.
"Kitty will kill me,"
    she wailed--
Kitty was Jean's mother.
    I don't remember what
Kitty said or did.
    But Mother put us
in the bath-tub
    with as much kerosene
as she could muster.
    I think she cried
as she scrubbed us--
    the entire time--
        and so did we.

We were somewhat green
for the rest of the summer.

PUNISHMENT

ॐ

My mother was a switcher,
  not a paddler,
and she preferred limber
  peach-tree switches,
or willow--but not the tips.
  She always sent me
to pick my own,
  knowing how it enhanced
    the punishment.
Sometimes I whined, apologized,
  and promised never
to transgress again;
  sometimes I returned switchless,
saying I couldn't break it off--
  in which case she sent me back
    with a paring knife.
I always hated to hand it over,
  remembering quite clearly
the sharp cutting sting,
  three or four times repeated.
I have no idea now why
  it did not serve as a deterrent;
my Dad had only to look
  disappointed with me,
    and I was chastened.

This summer day had started out
  with her complaining that
I never had my nose out of a book.
  So I thought I would give
her the pleasure of my company
  all day long--close company.

I walked a foot behind her
  everywhere she went--
anticipated what she was
  going to reach for
and reached it first.
  Sometimes I mimicked her,
repeating exactly what she said,
  but softly and careful
not to use a sassy voice.
  (I kept hoping for a giggle.)
If she worked at the sink,
  I got my hands in it, too;
I followed her back and forth
  to the garbage can,
the back porch, the bathroom.
  Finally, having ignored me
long past what I had bet on,
  she whirled and stamped her foot:
"Thunder and mud!" she yelled.
  "You have deviled and tormented me
all day deliberately. Enough--too much!
  Go out and pick a switch--a stout one."
"A stout one," I mimicked.
  "Don't you have one saved
on top of the refrigerator?"
  I scuttled hastily out
  without looking back,
feeling her anger reaching after me.
  Outside, still simmering
with whatever possessed me that day--
  I spotted the clothes-line pole--
six or seven feet of sturdy
  one-by-three, notched at one end
and used to prop the clothesline up
  to keep the sheets from dragging.
Inspired, thrilled with the danger,

I grasped the pole,
propped the back door open
  and lugged it into the kitchen.
"Here, I said," (her back was to me)
  "You wanted a stout one!"
thrusting it at her.
  She stared at me, fury and
frustration igniting,
  burst into tears,
seized the clothes-line pole,
  strode to the back door--
and hurled it like a javelin
  over the garage.
It cleared it by a good two feet
  and stuck upright in the garden beyond.
I followed it out, running.
  And sat for hours, lunchless,
in the cave under the willow tree
  at the far side of the vacant lot
on the corner, wishing I had a book,
  and cataloguing my transgressions--
wondering if this time would trigger
  an abandonment by parents,
having heard about incorrigible children.
  I thought I had better go back,
at least by supper time,
  to request a reasonable punishment,
which I undoubtedly did not deserve.

I don't remember how or when
  we made up, my mother and I,
and it was some time later
  that I realized I was no longer
    being sent outside
        to bring back switches.

IN MY MOTHER'S KITCHEN

૪૭

It is early on an August morning
in my mother's immaculate kitchen.
   She has washed the breakfast dishes
and is watering the row of now-bloomless
   African violets lined up on glass shelves
across the open windows,
   already planning dinner.
Josephine, her neighbor from one street over,
   comes yoo-hooing in the back door
neat in a fresh housedress,
   escaping her unwashed dishes
and her musty, cluttered house.
   Josie fancies herself a poet
(she is president of PenWomen)
   and writes a column for the local newspaper.
She comes for a cup of good coffee
   several mornings a week;
she never learned to make good coffee.
   Her husband, Doc, a dentist,
comes nearly every evening
   just at supper-time, checks the oven,
nods, gets himself a glass of port
   from the decanter left for him
on the breakfastroom table
   and goes to sit in the red easy chair
in our den while we eat supper.
   He nods again on his way out.
This morning there's a one-egg
   yellow cake in the oven,
and the kitchen smells richly
   of bacon and coffee and cake.
Josie has to peek into the oven,
   gently easing the heavy door shut
so the rising cake won't fall.

She sighs as she sits down
　and reaches for her cup.

They are opposites, these friends--
　my mother small, wiry, buxom, quick--
compulsive, neat, and often fearful--
　shiny auburn hair wound in neat braids
on top of her head. A doer, not a thinker.

　Josie is soft, complaisant, a little plump,
slow-moving, and accepting of most human foibles--
　she has loose, wispy hair and is vaguely pretty.
Disdaining housework, she collects bric-a-brac,
　and though she can fix a few elegant dishes,
ordinary cooking is simply beyond her.
　Their only child, Bill, frequently
eats at our house--more often still
　during the summer when school is out.
He is the brother I never had,
　and I regularly wrestle him to a draw.
If I pull his hair I beat him.
　My mother thinks it unladylike
of me to sit astride a red-faced boy,
　my fingers firmly entwined
in his straight blonde hair.
　But Bill is a fine surrogate brother,
and I am glad my grades
　are better than his most of the time.
He likes to annoy me by saying,
　"I am a philosopher;
I think out the *why of things.*"
　Josie likes to play the cultivated lady
to my Mother's "just a country girl."
　She plays symphonies on their record player
when Doc is gone and reads her poems aloud.
　But she also knows how to make
my mother feel good, too:
　"Tommie, my land, it's eight o'clock

on a blistering morning and here
    you are in a spotless kitchen
with a cake in the oven.
    It would take two maids two weeks
to shine up my kitchen like this,
    and they'd never make it smell this good.
I beg Fred to get me a cleaning lady--
    we always had servants at home, you know."
My mother, her eyes on her cup, says,
    "You're missing something
about my spotless kitchen, Josie.
    There's a very dead mouse in a trap
behind the stove. I'm leaving him
    for Leo--his job, and he knows it."
Josie doesn't check on the mouse.
    She sets her cup down
on the porcelain-top table
    ands scurries out the back door.
"Ta-ta," she calls,
    "I must be on my way--
a luncheon to go to, you know,
    and my column to write. Ta-ta."
My mother sits down again to her coffee,
    aware that, now, in the kitchen's heat,
the mouse-smell is noticeably
    overwhelming the cake smell.
She smiles a small smile
    and decides to clean the bathroom next.

HOMEPLACE

Down in Sourwood Hollow,
where the sun rises late
over the ridge-rims,
   the phoebes' name-calling
and the cardinals' "chit-chit"
   still declare
the habit of cheerful living.

Set foursquare within
   the rounding years,
the old homestead cabin
   centers the hollow--
shelter and home
   for a century and half another.

George Curtis chose this spot
   across the creek
from the clear-water spring.
   He cut the great grey logs,
hewed them with broad-axe,
   smoothed them with foot-adze,
notched them deeply and true--
   raised and fit them together
at the corners
   like hands clasping.
Mud chinking he heartened
   with small wedges of stone
to seal out the winds and rains
   that swept through the hollow.
Creekstone he used for the chimney,
   limestone for the hearth,

cedar shakes for the roof.
  An iron kettle swung
over the hearth fire
  where his wife Nancy cooked.
They furnished the two rooms
  sparsely with beds and tables,
generously with nine children.

Their son Tandy and his Nancy raised
  their ten children--
nine girls and a lone boy--
  on the puncheon floors
and corn-shuck pallets in the loft.
  He added a cook-shed on the back
and built a sawbuck table
  big enough for twelve.
They grew tobacco and corn
  and a big kitchen garden.
They had a pair of mules,
  two cows, some pigs and chickens,
and three hounds for hunting.

Here they worked and laughed
  and cursed and ate and loved.
The cabin and the hollow
  contained their growing up
and growing old.
  Homestead was homeplace.

Others have since come
  to the hollow,
claimed the cabin as home,
  thought they could hear the voices
of their predecessors.
  They added on to the cabin,
laid down white-ash floors,

cut a new road in.
Voices and bird-calls still
  resound through the valley.
Deer and wild turkeys and foxes
  find sanctuary.
The spring has long since
  gone underground,
but rhododendrons bloom
  across the creek,
and the hawks
  keep watch overhead.

The old pine-log cabin
  stands sturdy witness to
the secret of survival.

RIDE INTO DARKNESS

In autumn dusk
　　you rode sidesaddle
on our old sorrel mare,
　　and I, shivering,
sat astraddle her rump--
　　short legs too short
to grasp her sides
　　stuck out like puppet's legs.
And in the windy dark,
　　stockings slipped down
and knickers up
　　leaving bare flesh
for rising wind to lap at.
　　You pulled our Molly up,
slid down and took off your shawl
　　and wrapped an end
around each leg.
　　I clung more closely
when you were again
　　in saddle, hiding my
face in your back--
　　feeling you shiver.
You talked to hold back
　　the cold and nameless
terrors of the road.
　　I clung and trusted
you to bring us safely home.
Now I, a man grown old,
　　face chiller winds
and longer rides into
　　the pathless dark.
And you, my sister,
　　where are you?
　　　Out in the pathless dark, too?

JULIA

&

She must have
clung
to such
a slender
thread,
though family
and friends
and lover
thought her
attached
securely
by strong
cords
of gaiety
and
love.

Afterwards
they discovered
she couldn't cope
with everydayness
and bills
and love's
responsibilities,
and so she
ended by
clinging
to a hose
and
she left
the motor
running.

PLOWING

Behind the sweating mule
he plunges through curling furrows,
hard hands grasping plow handles,
thick chest straining shirt-buttons.
He flaps the reins and hallos
to old Bess:
  Keep it up, old girl,
  we've nearly licked this last piece.
  Ma'll be glad we're done...

**They kneel beside his bed
and put their arms across
to hold him down.**

Take her down to the water trough
and fetch her feed bucket,
   he calls out,
She done a fair day's work.
It's all ready now for dragging,
soon's it dries out a day or two.
Then we can get to planting.
Lord, I'm bone dry.

**They offer him water,
but he sweeps them aside.**

  Let's get us a drink,
he says,
and kneels by the spring
in the cool of the trees.
  The water, cold enough
to hurt his teeth,
is nutty-sweet.
  Again he leans over,
fills the gourd-dipper

and pours it over his head--
shakes his head, flinging droplets.

Hold his head, they say,
he'll hurt himself.

He sits back on his heels,
knees and shirt collar wet,
cool water trickling down his back--
throws his chin up
and smells the rich deep woods-scent,
closes his eyes and rests.

Is he going now? they ask.
Breathing like that,
it'll tear his throat out.
It's shaking the bed--look.

He relishes the breeze
across his sunburnt neck
when he bows his head.
  Thank you, Lord,
    he says,
  for this good work
  and this good mule.

  Bess, oh, my Bess,
    he whispers now,
  you see to Bess.

Who is Bess? they ask.
Grandma's name was Mary Lee.

  Got to get me up,
    he says,
  and go inside.
He claps his knees and rises.

Pull up the sheet,
they say,
he's gone.

THE LETTER

&

On fragile lined tablet paper
    written carefully in pencil,
dated Sun. night Feb. 26, 33,
    two days before my grandmother
unexpectedly entered widowhood:

    Dear All,
Have had company since early
Saturday afternoon. Henry,
    Izema and family all (except for Victor)
came and seemed to have a good time.
    Dorothy broke out in great big hives
and kept on throwing up, but Izema
    never did take her down to see Dr.,
she thought she surely would get better.
Joe and I went to Branch Boardman's
    funeral Thursday afternoon.
Amanda was taking on pretty bad,
    but then she's got those five children
that have given them so much grief.
They heard from Elisabet once, from Texas.
    She asked them to forgive her,
if they couldn't to forget her.
    Said she would be far from that place
by the time they got her letter.
    Remember when Pap had to light out
to St. Louis after Joe to bring him back
    when he ran away and got pneumonia?
We then went to see Mrs. Thomas.
    She has been in bed several days now
with trouble in her legs.

She spends her time working
a jigsaw puzzle Frances gave her
    and doesn't seem to fret
about things getting done or cooking.
    Troop finally moved last Wed.,
Clark is laying a new floor
    but don't seem in much of
a hurry to get moved in.
    I made Dorothy a pair of pillows
and a silk comfort.
    She seemed real pleased with them,
since Mary and Elizabeth had theirs some time.
    Pappy is reading while I write this.
Joe is reading too. Seems like
    he couldn't find a date this week.
Henry came Saturday morning late.
    Wanted to take us to Lexington
to supper and then to a show.
    Pap said he wasn't able
after chasing down the cows
    that broke through the fence again
but would stay to home with the children.
    We had an early dinner,
then Henry, Ize and I went on
    to town and took in a show--
Jim Tulley's Laughter in Hell
    some wild show Pap wouldn't have liked.
Went by Lizzie's house--no one was there--
    and staid awhile then on to home.
For supper, I'll give you what we had--
    beans, onions, corn dodgers, and
inch-thick steak, fried potatoes,
    apple sauce, biscuits, coffee,
new potatoes Henry brought, new beans,
    strawberries Izema brought (huge, nice)
and apples and oranges and hickory nut cake.

And I forgot, some of Izema's beef ham--
it sure was fine.
　　For breakfast had fried shoulder,
scrambled eggs, fried mush, biscuits,
　　coffee, jellies, and pear preserves.
I sent some of every thing home with Henry.
　　Wish you could have been here with us.
　　Am not going to write to Beanjie
and Barbara tonight--too tired,
　　and Pap is going up to bed.
It sure has been a fine day here.
　　　　Love to all, Mother

P.S. Write to Amanda soon.
　　It sure is hard to be a widow
without no warning or signs
　　and not have your man
and nothing coming in.

　　Tell Ann the children
brought Pappy a jigsaw puzzle.
　　Maybe I can get him to work on it,
but he says he don't have the time.

GROWING OLD

Come on up on the porch
and take a seat--
   your chair's all broke in.
I was settin here waitin
   for you this evenin.
Been thinkin all them old
   thoughts that go with the fall
of the year--you know them thoughts?
   Seems like a day or two ago
I was sixteen and marryin Jesse D,
   and havin that baby that
didn't get started good and
   worryin I might never have one a'tall.
Well, I had two, as you know
   because I've told you, and was carryin
Willis when Jesse D. died, and then
   I was nineteen and a widow.
You know all this, but I been
   thinkin today that there is no way
to know what the Lord has in mind
   for a body--maybe you got a better idea--
so I better say onliest for me, I reckon.
   Still don't, and that's a fact.
But it is time for me to think
   on what it is I've done
in my life and all, and what
   there is still for me to do.
I go over and over in the middle
   of the night what I got left to do,
and I wish He'd speak right out
   and tell me plain so I could get to it.

You're still young, and you got time
    to figger it out, but I'm not
what I used to be and "going downhill fast,"
    as Aunt Matt used to say--specially
when I'm out at the woodpile choppin
    or tryin to squat to pull beans;
the inside of me feels young,
    I look out of my eyes real young,
but that old tired mirror over the sink
    tells me the truth like it or no,
and my hair gets thinner and grayer by the day--
    you don't remember them thick auburn
braids I wore up on my head,
but I can recollect the weight of them
    and the shine and how I brushed them out.
Now I just give it a twist and put a pin in.
    And I look down at these old bunion-feet
and think of all the times I wanted
    to go dancin and Pa wouldn't let me.
Wish I had gone anyhow--
    dancin don't hurt nobody.
I thought me and Jesse D. would get away
    from this old holler and do some things
to think on the rest of our lives.
    But raisin three on my own
didn't leave me time for dancin.
    Now-- you go dancin while you got the time
and legs for it--don't wait, like me.
    Leaves fall off, and the mists come on,
and the snow and ice start in,
    and another year is gone--yes, gone.
Don't think it ain't gone,
    for I set here thinkin that rememberin
ain't nearly as good as plannin,
    and harvestin ain't as good
as plantin--no, not really--no.

Feels like the end, not the start, you see.
So I work all day round this old place
  and think and save up things to tell you
in case you chance to come on up to see me,
  and then I'm not certain just what it is
exactly that I need to say to you,
  but right now I'll bite off
a mighty big chew and
  tell you flat out just now
what I know for certain sure--
    there's a whole heap more
      to growing old
        than growing ugly.
You know I tell you true.

A BITTER END

When she found herself
    too frail to live alone,
she moved from her
    leaky log cabin
to her brother's
    which was more tightly
chinked and soundly roofed.
    He, the only male,
with nine sisters,
    who spoiled him,
had not really
    survived the war,
and now he sat, silent,
    in the chimney corner
and watched
    as she struggled
to keep them fed
    and warm.
Once in a while
    she railed at him,
but she had to hoard
    her strength
to boil their coffee
    and cook their mush.
He did not offer
    to help her
in her weakness
    as she dragged in
fallen tree limbs
    and shoved them,
butt-end first,

into the ash-filled
fireplace
    to feed the meager fire.

Neighbors found them there
    close to the cold hearth--
he staring and stiff
    in his chair
and she on her knees
    still clutching the charred end
of an oak-tree branch
    and frozen stiff
and the cabin door
     banging in the winter wind.

They talked about
    how he was always
a little "quare"
    and how he hated
to be bossed
    and how Margaret
was always known
    to be the bossy one.

In the end
    her nieces willingly deeded over
her fifty acres to a man
    who offered to pay
their burial costs.

TIME HEALS

&

Can't say I agree with you--
    leastways, not entire.
You take a good look at my Em, there.
    She ain't never been the same
since our girl was took.
    She was a kind of wild one,
but Em loved her better'n life
    and held faith in her--
in her turning out good after all.
    She might not look
no different, my Emily,
    but she ain't light
on her feet no more.
    She goes to meeting just the same,
but she don't sing.
    When I ask her how she's coming--
fine as a frog hair, says she,
    but there's no shine to it no more.

Regarding what you said
    about time healing all--
see them big old white oaks
    yonder, along the fence line?
See where the old barbed wire's
    done bit into their flesh
where it was stapled on
    when they was saplings?
It's in there deep,
    not just the outside bark.
Them trees kept on living
    and kept on growing

after them fence strands
   was stapled to them,
but they just growed over
   that wire, barbs and all.
There's wounds, deep ones,
   and the barbs is still there,
but they've kind of sealed over
   and you sure couldn't pull them out.
But they ain't the same--
   they're bad scarred,
and they been changed, no doubt--
   survived, but the barbs're still there.

That's my Em, I reckon.
Time helps, God knows,
   but it don't heal all.

LOST DOG

A flash of white
  catches at the
corner of my eye.
  Weeks after,
I swing my head
  from side to side,
searching.
  I see him lie
sleeping in the corner
  or waiting at
the back door
  to come in.
And far down
  the graveled lane
where it disappears
  into pines and maples,
I see him trotting
  homeward
like a warrior stallion--
  slim white legs
and dainty feet;
  caparisoned in burnished black,
white ruff gleaming,
  plumey tail high-held
like a banner;
  ears erect and
eyes alight with pride
  of many battles won
and marvelous adventures
  in unknown lands--
coming home assured
  of hero's welcome
and prodigal's return.

WHERE THE PINWHEEL TURNS

Many are dead
    in that windy place
on the flat ridge-top
    at the dwindled end
of the gravel road.

Many are dead
    in that lonely place
next the ruined church
    and the windowless school
where hymns echo low
    and the chorus of sums
drifts lost in the cedars.

Many are dead
    and some in rows
with lichened limestones
    measuring out
the sunken lengths
    in the withered grass.

Many are dead
    and no one comes.
But on the farthest side
    at the edge of the woods
is a little dirt mound
    where a toy tractor waits
and a plane
            and a truck
and a shabby wet bear,
    and a pinwheel turns

in the wind
        in the wind.

There's a stone
   with a name and
a single day's date,
   And a pinwheel turns
in the wind
       in the wind
a pinwheel turns
       in the wind.

BELIEVING

&

When I was very little,
there was a huge old man,
with white hair and a big belly,
   who lived next door
and came out, like the troll
in The Billy Goats Gruff,
   to call to me:
Come here, little girl!
I want to eat you.
I'll pin your ears back
and grease you good
and swallow you whole!
   Come here, little girl!
I am hungry. Come here!
I need a good snack!

                    I always ran away, of course,
                    with his big laugh following me.
                    My father said,
                       Never mind,
                    he is only teasing you.
                    You don't believe him, do you?
                       Then I rolled out of bed one night
                    and broke my collarbone
                    and had to wear my arm
                       bound across my chest
                    with a big hot heavy body-cast
                       above the waist.

One day I decided
to go out to stand by the fence
   this time to wait for him--
for the giant to come out to get me.
I felt very brave because,
   when he tried to swallow me down,
I'd surely stick in his throat now--
       wouldn't I?

ODDITIES
&

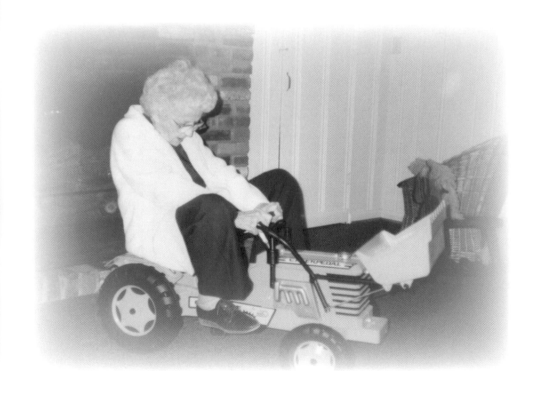

CHANCE ENCOUNTER

&

After this morning
I will always wonder
about the bent-over
     little old lady
wearing a red suit
and a lime felt hat
peering through
     the steering wheel
and driving
a dark-purple hearse
with lavender window curtains
     on a side street
       in front of
         a health club.

BEN'S POEM
OR
COUNTRY PREACHER'S WARNING

&

Woe be to ye
who callaripeth around
and walketh the roads
drinking whisky
and cavorting
with sorry women
for ye shall come
to an uncertain end
and that without notice.

JACKIE KENNEDY: A DREAM

I was off somewhere
    traveling with some group
and we were stopping off
    by some ocean.
I was as usual
    trying to repack my suitcase
and discovering all that
    I had left behind
that I needed
    to have brought along,
and things I didn't need.

When I stepped out into the sun
    and stiff sea-breeze,
there she was--
    Jackie Kennedy herself
in her little pillbox hat
    and a full-skirted dress.
And the first thing I noticed
    was: she hadn't shaved her legs--
under her stockings
    were long black hairs.
And as she held onto her hat
    and tried to hold down
her skirt in the wind,
    I saw she was wearing
a garter belt and stockings
    and I thought, she doesn't shave
her legs and she wears stockings
    on those elegant legs.

And then I thought;
    she is still young
and this is before the days
    of pantyhose.

SUPERMAN: A DREAM

&

There you are
in church
sitting beside me
clutching the lapels
of your suit jacket
together.
Are you cold? I ask.
No. Then what is wrong
with your shirt?
Nothing, you say,
and fling open your coat,
flashing a chartreuse
tee shirt with a pulsating yellow S.
Superman! I say.
Don't I wish, you say.
Then your chest balloons up
while the organ's introit
swells and swells.

AFTER-IMAGE

∞

On the padded operating table,
   strong lights penetrate the blue
cloth drape that covers my face,
   except for the eye
they are working on
   (that eye kept open
by a plastic speculum).
   And the burning eye
of the surgical microscope
   is fixed unblinkingly
on that open defenseless eye
     I cannot blink.

Later, eye cleaned out,
   reattached, sewed up,
and covered with a patch--
   still anaesthesia-numbed--
a bright-dark round spot appears
   at the bottom edge of vision--
blue, large, and back-lighted
   by a corona, the very replica
     of a sun's eclipse--
moving as my eye moves.
   The surgeon seems relieved
I do not report it
   as being in the center.

All day and night
it drifts at vision's edge
   behind my closed and
     bandaged eye,

a strange and scary beauty--
    artifact of surgery,
permanent or temporary.

    Next morning it is gone,
and when I tell the surgeon
    examining my tender eye,
he professes great relief,
    pronouncing it now
        "just-an-after-image"
and "thank-God-not-a-retinal-burn,"
    which scars, he says, for life,
        obscuring vision.

And I had to think then of life's
    after-images
            seared on memory--
    some beautiful as an eclipse,
            some scarring as a burn,
    and some--a few--
            dead center.

RED BIRDS

My air is fraught with red birds
   this March-windy morning--
whether five or fifty,
   I cannot know.
Flashing , weaving, bombing,
   landing for a nano-second
on the trees and bushes
   outside all my windows,
caucusing momentarily
   in the holly tree--
a manic spring circus--
   and probably with sex
on their little minds--
   zooming straight up,
dropping straight down,
   with flaunts of black bibs
and crests, flipping tails,
   they leave criss-crossing
crimson contrails in the fervid air.

All day male cardinals are
   everywhere I look,
though they are single now--
   erect and arrogant
   on their high perches.

At dusk a solitary female
primly feeds on ground-seed

LADY WITH BOUND FEET

Like a twisted juniper bonsai,
    centuries in the making
pruned and bent into artistic
    configuration,
the old woman with black-dyed hair
    balances on her tiny velvet-slippered feet
while her grown son
    takes her photograph on the Great Wall.
Somberly she poses, impassive
    as a miniature mannequin

in her white quilted tunic
    and her black silk trousers,
propped up, with her stunted feet
    turned outward for balance.
Ancient and ageless
    against the panorama of the wall
built centuries before to turn back
invaders,
    preserve a culture,
she is a living anachronism---
    like the bonsai,
pruned and bent for aesthetic goals,
    planted deep in China's soil,
forever hobbled,
    preserved for posterity
to admire
        for endurance.

LEAN INTO THE WIND

Oh, the courage
  have you, will you,
will you lean
  into the wind
  and let it--
  will you let it--
hold you up?
  Will you, can you
thrust yourself
  out into the gale,
into the buffeting,
  into the tossing air--
even with your buttons
  buttoned up?
Will you trust
  enough
to lean,
  to lean
into the wind
  and let it--
will you let it--
  hold you up?

Oh, the courage
  have I, hope I,
    to lean,
to lean
  into the wind
and let it--
  oh, to let it--
    hold me up.

SOURWOOD AND OTHER LOVES

&

SONG FOR SOURWOOD HOLLOW

When you go home
   to Sourwood Hollow,
back to green Kentucky hills,
   all you have to do
      is call--
and I will follow--
      follow you home
            to Sourwood Hollow.

Name, oh, name
   lift of the ridges,
      cup of the hollows,
   dogwood, redbud
      cedar and pine,
   slow-moving streamlets,
      clear-water pond,
   carved limestone bluffs,
      soft southern sky.

Call, oh, call,
   and I will follow.
I'll set my feet
      on the rock-ridge road
            down into Sourwood Hollow.

SHEDDING

Our valley sloughs
    its winter skin
oh, so gradually,
    rubbing up against cloud-ribs
and brown-boned ridges,
    shedding dead old leaves
and twigs and branches--
    emerging at last,
sleek and shiny
    and sensuous
and all-new again.

SPRING DRAGS HER HEELS

Spring drags her heels
this year
    and trips
over winter's frozen train.
    Undaunted,
she draws her warmest breath,
    lifts up her skirts,
and shakes them out
    in dandelions,
        violets,
            freshets,
                and bluebird wings.

FEBRUARY SPRING

Crocus yearns sunward,
  forsythia blazes butter-gold,
willow cascades green-gold,
  plum strings popcorn chains,
and red-bud punctuates pink.

But I am wary,
  for it is February.
I do not trust innocent robin's egg sky,
  eager daffodil, shy japonica--
not even thrusting tulip spear.
  I long to join the riot,
to shed my winter skin,
  to give in to universal borning,
without the dread of frost to come.

  But I remember Februaries.

RETREAT

  Old Winter fights
  a rear-guard action.
In his slow retreat
  he fires with shrewdest timing
his final rounds
  of frost and hail,
leaving behind
  a blighted trail
of blackened fruit-blossoms
  and frozen daffodils--
carnage worthy
  of a victor.

HARBINGERS

&

We balance on winter's cusp, or spring's:
    phoebes call at daylight's edge,
the faintest blush is on the maples;
    I mark lilacs' pointed tight-green buds,
and daffodils' hopeful spears here and there,
    crocus sun-yellow in two bouquets,
and a single blue flower in the winter grass.
    Bloodroot and trillium are biding their time,
but partridgeberry shows bright red berries
    like gems set among green shiny leaves.

The orchard's still barren and waiting,
    though the bees, hive-clustered, dully hum.
No rumor of green in the dun fields,
    but the creek's running full and brown
after the night's long insistent rains,
    and the willows are coming yellow.
The sky is filled with low gray
    movering clouds; the air is soft and raw.
Somewhere deep within,
    I feel a push toward spring.

    Then we hear them--honking--
two great Canadian geese--
    just under the clouds, honking
and flapping their way to the lake
    up at the top of the hollow,
magnet-pointed toward a nesting place,
    themselves both time and season.

Then, right then--spring is a certain hope.

SQUATTER'S RIGHTS

&

When I opened up
   the bluebird's weathered box
and thrust in my hand
   to clean it out
for this new season,
   I closed upon
         a tiny furry body
quivering at my touch--
   looked in and saw
two big black eyes
   belonging to
         a flying squirrel
fearfully expecting
         eviction.
I quickly shut the box
   and, quivering too,
stepped away,
   content to honor
         squatter's rights.

NO ONE WILL KNOW

No one but us will know
   the old fence row is clean at last--
that bit of fence just past
   the creek, along the bank.
We cut the weeds and brambles,
   pulled loose the honeysuckle vines,
chopped off the slender sumac stems.
   We cleared thick clumps of fescue
from around the bases
   of weathered locust posts,
pulled taut and nailed the tangled
   skeins of rusty barbed-wire fence.

It was a sunny January day,
   a January thaw, they'd say.
Somehow it made some special sense
   to clean away the last year's growth
(suppose it were a corner of our lives
   we could clean out and clear away just once)
between the next snow that will come
   and the fresh new season's growth.
It truly matters not a whit to us
   that no one else will care or know
that we cleaned up an old fence row.

THE VOW
&

On this blue-sky day
   I have vowed
never to forgive him
   for plowing up
the daffodils around
   the old house-site
(down in the lower meadow
   where the two little creeks
come together)
   to make himself
a new tobacco-bed.

BETRAYAL

The old stone fence grew
   out of the ground
which birthed it;
   limestone, flat and rectangular,
stone upon stone,
   leaning into each other,
mortarless but sturdy,
   as generations and seasons
flowed over and under it --
   rhythm inexorable
as ocean's beat.

The honeysuckle grew
   free and fragrant
upon the fence
   according to the season's whims.
Its tendrils penetrated
   unsuspecting crevices like doubt
and slowly had their way --
   camouflaged by siren-scent.

In growing time, green fingers
   were at work separating stones
wedged tight as custom --
   moving imperceptibly, steadily --
shifting merest millimeter
   until, one winter's night,
in frost-heave time,
   small avalanche of stone:
bastion breached and
   Troy betrayed again!

SOWERS
&

He goes out today
in high anticipation--
   my weekend farmer--
to harrow a meadow field
   and sow sweet clover
for his bees to graze.
   And I, alone
with the almost-springtime
   outside my window,
      content myself
with harrowing old ideas
   and sowing fresh images
sweet as any clover seed,
   hoping in season
      to attract
         some sippers
of my own.

BLACK-VELVET BEE

There's a great fat
  gold-banded, black-velvet bee
drinking deep from the
  dusty golden cup of a daffodil.
I stroke him boldly
  with a finger-tip,
but he sips on,
  undistracted
from his sweet debauchery.

Oh, would I could strike
  a mother-lode
    as rich, as golden--
      as worthy of devotion.

HAWK-SHADOW

Bird-song ceased
   when the hawk's
fierce shrieks pierced
   the summer-morning sky.
We heard the cry
   but blithely chattered on
until the awesome
   mighty hawk-shadow
      fell across us
      one by one.
We stopped our hoeing
   for a moment,
then began again--
   pensive, silent.

A STRAY BIT OF SUN

Caught in the bowl
　of the old kerosene lamp
is a stray bit of sun--
　　and there's no sun around.
In the rosy-gold oil
　　it glows with a canny light--
like a small core of passion,
　　like a primordial fire
trapped in amber,
　　like the seminal spark
preserved in liquid gold,
　　like a secret fire
to be handed down
　　generation to generation--
the quivering gleam and glow--
　　of all living things
since the creation
　　and before.

HIGH SUMMER

Tobacco's cut
   and ready for hanging.
the creek trickles
   slowly.
Trees are full
   and heavy-green.
Occasionally
   a single leaf
drifts down
   to nest
in thick dry grass.

Cicadas hum
   viola wings
and mists
   roll into hollows
early and
   linger late.
Goldenrod and
   purple ironweed
are man-tall
   in the meadows,
and whippoorwills
   call plaintively
for an early dusk.

Now is high summer--
   poised for the slide
      into autumn.

Fifty is high summer.

AUGUST NIGHT

Thin darkness seeps
through the ridgetop trees
  down into the hollow
and slowly thickens.
  Night sounds swarm
around the cabin,
  and a whippoorwill's call
startles--repeats, repeats.
  Fireflies fleck the dark
  like grindstone sparks,
  and a moon-sliver
is slung above the ridge.
  A shifting breeze brings
  sharp-sweet scent
  of grass new-cut
in the near small meadow
  where tall purple ironweed,
goldenrod, and pink joe-pye
  wait uncut along the fence-rows.
  Starshine sifts over tobacco
  yellowing in the field,
and earth's pulse slows
  to a steady beat.
    Perfect end-time could be now,
      coming easy and slow
      in a heart-stroke of time,
    homing in on the whipporwill's cry.

OLD BARN

The old barn hunkers down
  against the hill
leaning as if it meant to last
  another hundred years.
The rusty-red tin roof
  is frayed-edged as an old straw hat
and its charcoal weathered boards
  are as ragged at the bottoms
as a work-hand's jeans.
  Blackberry brambles grow in
and out the crevices to
  bloom and bear each season.
In stripes of sunlight
  molder unkempt heaps
of old fruit jars and bedsteads,
  odd bits of wood and harness
and tobacco sticks.

Old Tan Curtis carried
  on his shoulder
a single board a day
  from the sawmill
where he worked,
  in Clay City,
until he had a stack
  he judged sufficient
to start his barn.
  He had peeled the poles
and hewed the beams
  beforehand, in readiness.
He and his only son

and his nine daughters
put up the great corner posts,
    set firm on good square stones
and braced them strong enough
    to last his lifetime--
before he nailed on the boards
    and roofed it, nailed on the tin,
and made the great square doors.
    In it he housed his cows
and hung tobacco
    and stored his moonshine
until he died--
    and after him, his son.
Now, leaning only slightly,
    like an old man bracing

against the wind,
the old barn hunkers down
    as if he means to stay
another hundred years.

SEPTEMBER'S SONG

જીજી

The dark is flecked
    with sound tonight,
confetti-bright and variegated.
    The dark is crowded;
the hills press close,
    the sky stretched taut
and random-pricked
    where myriad stars shine through.
Cicadas orchestrate
                September's song,
and the wind laps
    drying corn leaves
with a raspy tongue.
    Autumn slips
                into Sourwood Hollow
on a moonless night
    when the stars are bright
and the wind is restless
    and the creek the tiniest
                thread of sound.
This night breathes
            a reverent requiem
                to summer.

WHIPPOORWILL

Just at the feathered
edge of dusk,
the whippoorwill begins
    his plaintive call.
  It cannot be a song to woo
    his lady love;
it has a stern discordant note.
    Perhaps he mourns
the loss of light
    or warns of coming dark.
Whip-poor-will, whip-poor-will,
    he cries again, again,
and then abruptly ceases
    as the lid of night
        is sealed.
We wait to hear his one last call,
        and, failing,
know again the deep dark
    texture of another night
        and of that final night
and are forewarned.

DUSK

*Dusk comes down
over Sourwood Hollow
like a soft-grey dove
settling over her nest
fluffing her feathers,
subsiding to rest.*

OWNERSHIP

I always did admire
a creek,
especially a small one,
a
conversational
creek
that wanders
through
a hollow,
conversing
through the days
and
nights and
seasons.
Once I thought
I'd like to own
a creek.
But now I say
I own a piece of land
that has a creek
meandering through it.
So, though I walk
along it and admire
its cheerful dialogue
and envy its blissful
lack of responsibility,
I have no doubts
concerning ownership--
no doubts at all.

HIATUS

Just at the edge of autumn,
  the sunflower
droops its heavy head,
  and the striped kershaws
hide among the weeds and vines.
  Shadow-fingers reach
across the meadow
  behind the barn,
and the creek's
  slow syllables are stilled.

The hollow seems hushed
  and waiting,
like a deer
  lifting its head from grazing,
   attentive,
poised in the brief hiatus
  between day and dusk--
   just at the forest's edge,
  and at summer's nether verge

METAMORPHOSIS

&

This early frost
brings down the leaves
that still seemed summer's.
Green on the still-full maple,
they metamorphose to yellow
floating down
like butterflies--
like gold-finches touching down
on crystallized green grass.

Tomorrow
they will be brown
and desiccated--
brown
as blasted dreams,
sere
as hope abandoned.

Faith cannot keep their yellow,
nor yet restore their green.

OUT OF SEASON

Late October, and a windy day
wind runs through the trees
              like water
goldenrod and blue-aster time
ironweed and joe pye
              fading now
daffodil and lilac-time
              world-turns away
cloud shadows race and shift
              kaleidoscope of sun
                and shade
but here, among the weeds
  in my abandoned garden
I glimpse low shine of purple
  and bend to find
a violet, short-stemmed,
  and only one--
but undoubtedly a violet--
  April brave
in my cupped October hands.

RICHES TO RAGS

All summer through, the hills,
   like prosperous burghers,
waxed plump and sleek.
  They clustered round
    the hollow's rim--
     gregarious.
Now, in mid-December,
  the ridges stand separate, aloof,
withdrawn, as poor men stand,
  ribs and backbones showing,
    quivering in the winds,
     their summer finery
in tatters at their feet.

GINGKO GOLD

We had the season's
  first hard frost
    last night,
and on this silver-sifted
  morning,
    highlighted
      in a shaft of sunlight,
the timeless gingko tree
  rains ancient gold
    into a golden pool
     too beautiful
      to step in.
It is the only gold around--
  a fountain, upside down
    and spraying gold--
     unspendable
and unspeakably
  valuable
    to behold.

ABORTED AUTUMN

The rains came too early this fall,
   splatting the leaves from the trees--
pasting them to the ground
   in a child's collage of primary color,
shattering the grand design
   into stained-glass shards
upon the withered grass.
   When at last the sun came out,
it shone upon the remnants
      of an autumn.

EXPIATION

Nature seems weary,
   late in November,
and has foregone
   her leaves
and relinquished
   her flowers.
As if in premonition
   of jeopardy or death,
she wishes to strip bare,
   to rid herself
of her possessions
   and superfluity--
to present herself naked
   to the cleansing flagellations
of fey wind and rain and snow.
   In deprivation, then,
and vulnerable,
   she stands alone, aloof,
resigned and stolid,
   awaiting
her annual expiation.

PEACH TREE

We gave up on it and cut it down.
The old peach tree was mostly dead.
   This year it put out only
a few slim green leaves
   at the very ends
 of the topmost branches.
   But last year it surprised us
and, like Abraham's old wife, bore--
   five small speckled peaches,
hard and green, but almost incredibly sweet.

   It was a tough old tree;
the chainsaw screamed
   as the sawdust flew.
It gently toppled over,
   its branches amputated,
and leaned into the hill's slope.
   We told ourselves we could plant
two more young trees now
   in the new orchard thriving
in the old orchard site.
   But new trees are too young to bear,
as the old one was too old.
   So there is a waiting time,
a vulnerable space, with no fruit
   expected, and few blossoms.
We counted the rings: sixty-four.
   Someone had planted it in
this hillside orchard plot
   in front of the cabin
and watched it grow

and had picked and eaten
long before we were born.
    And someone else, his grandfather maybe,
had hewed the logs and raised the cabin
    and planted an orchard
before he was born.

We will cut up the old peach tree
    to burn in the cabin fireplace
and offer up prayers
    to the bright flames
for those of us
    who must, willy-nilly,
be for now the sad cutters-down
    and the dreaming planters.

METAPHOR

&

Outside,
within the cabin's
    encircling lampglow,
I stand, this warm December night,
    to mark a New Year's
slim fingernail moon
    and a single star
hung just above
    like specimen jewels
against black-velvet cloth.
    Then I walk away
until, in the seminal darkness
    at the wood's edge,
I look up again,
    and like a revelation
behold the sky
    millioned in stars
as if virgin-created
    and only for me--
light-cultured
    but cradled
        in darkness.

WINTER MORNING

&

Darkness thins and thins
   'til shapes emerge
out of the covering blackness.
   Like charcoal sketches,
the old barn with its
   lone sentinel cedar,
muted with mist,
   and the woodshed
and the smokehouse
   stand forth--
discovered once again.
   The slumbering hollow
gives in to morning
   as almost liquid light
spreads like incoming tide
   along the valley floor.

Winter wheat, new-planted
   in summer's tobacco patch
surprises the sober landscape
   like sudden, unexpected joy--
coaxes hopeful green
   from quiescent, frost-bound land,
      like a long-guarded secret
         waiting to be told.

WINTER LANDSCAPE

It is a quiet landscape--
   a chiaroscuro of white
with grays and browns
   and dullest greens.
The woods on the ridge-tops
   are naked stems limned
against a pewter sky,
   and the old barn
is stark against the white
   of the meadow rising
to meet the woods.
   It is a silent world
with no bird calls and
   no breeze stirring laden limbs.

The bee hives along the creek
    are square-capped with snow,
and animal tracks leave
    delicate testimonials.
Inside the hives hums
    a subdued murmurous life,
while under the creek's
    frosted-glass ice
is a small quiet ripple
    of moving water.

It is a still life
    painted eons ago--
of a quiet hollow
    snow-bedded,
with a homestead log cabin
    and a corn crib and chicken house
and barns and sagging wooden gates
    and snow-covered ponds.
It seems remote,
    sealed away in time,
incapable of the green
    that is to come--
a white mask disclaiming
    the certain hope
        of blue skies
            and springing green,
        of birdsong
    and of freshets.

THE MEASURE

∽

The morning sun
   shows late and tentative
above the winter ridgetop,
   and early, glowing, slips
below the opposite hills.

We mark and savor
   the shorter sweetness
of December's day,
      measured out
like childhood Christmas's
   rock-crystal candy
to us who linger
   in Sourwood Hollow's
      quiet fastness.

I PITY YOU WHO HAVE NO SECRET PLACE

I pity you who have no secret place--
no mind's retreat, no haven for the heart.

I have a place to know, to be,
far within the blue and hoary mountains--
deep, deep hidden but for memory's reaching,
where flow the clear and rushing waters--
meeting, merging, changing--speaking--
surging down and round the shiny boulders,
around the green and mossy boulders--
slipping soft and sweetly in the shallows.

Can you see and feel and smell
the primal greenness of it all
ancient rhododendron leaning over
virgin poplars soaring skyward
moist and fecund earth-smell
sunlight slanting
talking, restless water
lambent, listening air?

Oh, I pity you who have no secret place,
no soul's sanctuary, no healing space.

MUSINGS
❦

SUFFERING FOOLS

My husband suffers fools
more gladly,
   and certainly
more graciously,
   than I do.
He can lead them back
from the brink
   of foolishness
without taking them
by the hand
   or succumbing
to the temptation
to push them over--
   as I do.

SISYPHUS-STONE

I wish I could lead
    a lyric life,
with time to kick a can,
    skip a stone,
lie in a hammock,
    pick a guitar.
But I carry
    my Sisyphus-stone
around with me--
    create mountains
to push it up--
    afraid to take my hands away,
not just for fear
    it will roll back on me,
        but that it will
            start a landslide--
                cover me up.

SHARING

*Like a dog
joyously
retrieving the stick
his master threw,
she brought
her treasures
home
to lay them at his feet
only to watch him
toss them away
again.*

SHAKE THE TREE

*A good man once said to me,
speaking about writing, actually,
"Shake the tree
until nothing else
falls off."
Well, I have done just that.
And all that's left
is
Love.*

PAIN

Pain's a great leveler.

Though it peaks
    and wanes,
it levels all,
    reduces all,
changes all--
wherever, whomever,
    whenever.
Ever.

OLD DOGS

Old dogs
    trying to learn
        new tricks
are fun
    to be around.

MEASURING

&

I shall henceforth
   measure my life
by dusks and dawns,
   daffodils and blowing snow--
not greetings and farewells,
   nor clock-tickings,
      nor birthdays.

LADY MOUNTAINS

&

Elegant lady mountains
   scarved in purple mist,
rich-furred with evergreens,
   watch, unimpressed,
the bourgeois seasons
   come and go.

HOSTAGES TO FORTUNE

ॐ

I agree
  that they who
   have children
yield up hostages
  to fortune
and spend their lives
  attempting to pay

the ransom.

GROWTH

ॐ

It is not a new thought
   that growth is painful;
I merely wonder why,
   when it is only natural
and there is no way
   to prevent it,
      except by dying.

And you surely
   must have heard
the hoary old one,
      saying,
dead at thirty-seven,
   buried at ninety-two.
I mentioned growth.

GREENER GRASS

Those who live
in the ivory tower
aspire to the common road,
while those of us
who roam the streets
and work the fields
long to avoid the traffic.

FATAL ATTRACTION

I have always cherished
a secret desire
to be fatally attractive
to someone other than
old men,
little boys,
…and dogs.

DRINKERS

&

There is a whole river to drink.
   Shall we sip it delicately
      here and there,
      spit out the distasteful
      and go on to another sample?
Or shall we drink
      in great thirsty gulps
      indiscriminately
         until we are ready to burst?
Shall we dabble fingers only,
      afraid of contamination,
         and refuse to drink at all?

There is a whole river
      still to drink
      whatever kind of drinker we are.

COMPUTER LITERACY

ॐ

It is a gauzy
   unsubstantial thing
which flocks to light
   on summer evenings,
forgetting its larval beginnings
   grubbing in the mud
of arithmetic and algebra.
                  Like mayflies.

COMMONPLACE PUDDLES

ॐ

Oh, leave us alone
   to wallow
in our commonplace
   puddles;
They are not deep enough
   to drown in
but quite sufficient
   to muddy us up.

COMMENTARY

&

At her age
she needed nothing,
  wanted little--
except someone
  to listen.
Mostly
    she talked
      to herself.

BALANCE

&

Fortunately
  the readers
and the bleeders
  of the world
are balanced out
  by the hoers
and the mowers.
  Or is it
the other way
  around?

A LITTLE KNOWLEDGE

I have always wondered
about that Pierian spring,
having discovered
        that sometimes
a *little* knowledge
        is kinder,
            more comfortable,
easier to live with--
        than a lot.

TO MY DAUGHTER

I suspect what matters most
is not things or people
        for whom the heart aches,
but those
        for whom it leaps.

LOOKING BACK

⁊

ANCESTORS

Mine is a short tale
of a mixed breed,
   seldom told, little discussed:
blue-eyed child of blue-eyed parents--
   Jew and Gentile--
resembling neither.
   Two who came
together
in love, abjuring
tradition.
   Bluegrass farmers
on one side,
Jewish merchants
on the other.
   Grandparents who
never met
or talked or
corresponded.
   Never the long
shadowy line
of ancestors
standing behind,
   never the "she-
takes-after,"
never the religion
thing mentioned.

A great grandfather
kept slaves
   in Plum Lick,
Kentucky,

and one farther back on the other side
   was a one-armed Rabbi from Alsace-Lorraine,
who came in through New Orleans.
   The rest seem lost in dailiness
not worth the telling.

   So I grew up as my own self
with all things possible or probable--
   no fail-safe of genes
to claim or to blame.
   Few stories, either, for comfort
or context or recounting--
   just those we are living ourselves--
making and keeping traditions--
   neither much wondering what really was,
nor thinking what might have been,
   but creating our legacy of family,
remembering our own brief history--
   becoming ancestors ourselves.

FIRST ANNIVERSARY

Autumn was more wanton then:
She shook her gypsy skirts
   and danced to the wild tambourines
      the wind shook.
The haze in the ruddy air
   and the gold and crimson leaves
were kind to the new raw grave.

This year autumn is subdued, forlorn;
   she stands in her gaudy garments
bedraggled and wet with rain--
      her dance is stilled.
 Rains soak the grass-covered grave
   where we stand and remember
and lay our flowers down
      in memory of shared love
         and autumns gone.

LAST RIDE HOME

&

His eyes, hospital-dimmed,
were gloried by
   the sun-saffrons
and the scarlets
   on that last ride home.
He said he could not remember
   a more brilliant autumn
as we slowly moved
   beneath the panoply.
So lavish a display
   dazzled his senses
and teared his eyes.
   Cherished with memories
of autumns past,
   we did not know
      it was his last ride home.

MY FATHER'S HANDS

My father's hands were broad and thick,
    the fingers not tapering--blunt--
with nails that were wide and thick:

strong, competent, ugly hands.
    (And he had narrow patrician feet.)
They were almost always rough
    and raw, because of the work he did
and all of the handwashing.

His hands could do anything:
    pen beautiful letters,
build heirloom furniture,
    glue back together the tiniest pieces,
do intricate wiring in small places,
    or fix anyone's machines.
Whatever was needed, they did.
    They were ambidextrous hands--
for eating, writing, using tools,
    and performing showman's feats.
They were for gentling puppies
    and babies, for holding hands,
for clinging to.
    I did not mind that they snagged my hair.

    Only during the last months of his life
did his hands become soft, fine-grained, and smooth.
    I sat and held and felt them,
marvelling, and wishing they were rough again.
      I feel them still.
      I always will.

UPKEEP

For you, there was just me,
   and a daughter,
but I always knew
   you never even wished for a son.
(You kept my trophies on your dresser,
   my poems in your drawer.)

You thought it marvelously
   rich and funny, then,
     that your only one
had somehow produced four,
   who chased about our house--
a pack of merry scalawags.

You would laugh and, hugging me,
   catch at them for a stolen kiss
(twenty quick years ago)--
   and, watching them, say to me:
You know, it's not the original cost,
   Chick, but the upkeep.

And, Dad, wherever you are,
   I want you to know
     how wrenchingly right
      you were.

HANDS SPEAK

&

I remember very little
about my father's mother,
except that she was a big woman
with bad feet
and curly, thin fine hair
(she had spit curls on her forehead)
and big raw hands.
She had servants every day,
so her hands weren't raw
from work.
She washed them
a hundred times a day--
slowly, methodically,
as if she were a surgeon.
She would sit on the
second-floor porch
and rock and talk
until she thought it was time
to wash her hands again.
She fretted because my hair
was long and thick and straight
and tried to curl it with papers
every time I went to see her.
Her hands would catch in my hair.

Though I cannot hear her voice,
her raw, tormented hands
speak to me.
Dare I hear?

SUNFISH

*It was childhood's blithest hour
    when I drew them
with a silken string
    glittering, glinting
from the shining shallow stream--
    small as the palm
of my small child's hand--
    like sun-flakes,
like stained-glass shards,
    like gold-grains,
shimmering, shedding
    drops of rainbow--
precious as golden ducats.
    With gold-leafed fingers
I carried them home
    as innocent fee-payment.

Mealed and fried--served up for lunch--
    the bone-filled morsels
        of my childhood we ate
            with tiny careful bites.*

RED AND YELLOW

&

It was a terrible mischance
   on a sun-rinsed springtime day.
I was playing jacks
   out in the cistern's shade
when fat white Lucy waddled by,
   leading her parade
of yellow-dandelion ducklings.
   In delight I started up,
stepped back one step
   and squashed a duckling
with a not-so-heavy heel--
   he had broken ranks.
Red blood ran
   from his yellow bill,
and nothing--
   not tears,
nor bloodstained cradling hands,
   nor a shoebox burial
with prayers
   and sweetpeas atop--
would make him right.

Hard lesson that.

JUNEBUG DAYS

Coffee smells like Junebugs,
   I say, not thinking,
and turn back the years
   like bookleaves
to fat brown Junebugs
   held prisoner
with a black thread
   tied to a hind leg
and whirled around my head.
   Its Junebug smell
and angry motor-buzz
   caught in my memory
with sticky legs
   and frantic rasp,
plucked out only now
   by coffee-fumes--
fat-brown, oily, rank.
   The Junebug motor
rattles on, stringing years
   on a thin black thread,
flinging memories
   round about my head--
Junebug days--
      sun-washed, grass-stained.

I can taste childhood
   on my tongue
   like Junebugs
   on my hands.

UBI EST?

∽

Where is she now--
   the skinny little girl
long-legged, knobby-kneed
      as a colt--
running barefoot,
   pigtails flying out behind,
along the sharp-edged
      slanted rocks
atop the stacked-rock fence?

It was a game she played,
   proud that her older cousins
couldn't do it,
   relishing her uncle's threat
      to tan her hide
if she dislodged his stones.
   But she, light and nimble,
could run all the way
   to the mailbox near the bridge
down on the pike and back
   without once touching ground.

   Where is she now,
that lithe tough-footed child?

   Drawn back to look aghast
at the unpainted old farmhouse
   and the breeched rock fences
spewed out into the tall brambles.

   She wants urgently
to get out of her stopped car--
      restack rocks
         sharp-edged
            as time.

FIRST MEMORY

Years later they told me that
　　I was only five days past two.
　But when I was six or seven
　　and someone asked what was
the very first thing I remembered,
　　it wasn't hard for me to sort it out:
I was in the parlor at Grannie's house--
　　　the cold red parlor
(unused, except at Christmas)--
　　with its crimson velvet chairs
and the hard brocade sofa
　　I was never allowed on,
and the Turkey carpet
　　and the out-of-tune piano.

On this cold February day
　　next to the front window
　　　　in the parlor,
there was a long silvery box
　　with a lid that was up,
sitting on some kind of legs,
　　and my Pappy was in it.
Just barely, I could peer over the edge.
　　I saw him asleep on a shiny white pillow,
white moustache soft and full,
　　hands folded across his good black-satin vest.
I pulled and tugged a chair over,
　　climbed in, and snuggled down
beside him, my head just under his chin.
　　They were horrified and loud
when they opened the parlor door
　　and saw me comfortably asleep
　　　　on Pappy's chest.

And they broke into my remembering:
   "You were in his coffin! His *coffin!*"
they said to me, voices loud again,
   aghast that I had remembered
what they had never told.

My first memory, and that of death,
   I treasure--the only memory of Pappy
that is truly mine--belongs just to me,
   the youngest grandchild,
who got my other memories
   from other's lips and letters
and faded sepia photographs.

I know now that he was
   wiry, strong, a quite-small man,
respected and substantial farmer,
   builder of rock fences still standing.
I have his left-handed scythe
   and his long crowbar my sons
      can barely lift.
I keep his black-velvet, plumed Mason's hat
   and his ceremonial sash and sword
in my cedar chest; these things I claimed.
   But he left to me, unwittingly,
   this first memory--a legacy
   of quiet, restful death
   unviolated by his leaving.
Though, in truth, now burdened
   with life's dubious wisdoms,
honed down by pain,
   I have not expected
that memories of deaths
   since that one--
and of deaths to come--
   will have been--will be--
so kind or so forgiving.

FLAT-IRON BOOKENDS

℘

Mondays, by sunup,
   the fire was going out back
under the old iron wash-kettle
   (big enough for me to hide in).
Alice shaved the bar of lye-soap in
   and poked the dirty work clothes
down and down in the bubbling water
   with a smooth-worn hickory hoe handle.
Ladies' clothes she washed carefully
   by hand in warm water
in the galvanized washtub
   on a small shiny washboard
and rinsed them through three waters.
   Clean clothes she pinned on lines
or draped over wire fences
   or spread out on the grass to bleach.
Then she made the starch
   or hand-sprinkled them
and added the bluing
   to get ready for the ironing.
She went from pump to washboard
   to stove to steaming kettle,
with me under her feet,
   "helping" her.

Tuesdays, she laid the ironing board,
   clean-cloth covered, across the backs
of two straight chairs
   and set the heavy flat-irons
on the cookstove to heat
   while breakfast cooked.

She started in as soon as she did up the pile of dishes.
   Hurry to the stove with a potholder;
      carry the hot iron over;
      test it with a spit-wet finger
  (hot enough if it hisses)
and start to iron that blouse
  smooth and dry, old Alice,
while the steam rolls off you
  and your broken-heel slippers
kick off.
  bear down hard, old Alice,
back and forth, back and forth.
  Wipe your dripping face
and arms on your clean rag;
  roll your sleeves up
and your stockings down.
  Take the cool iron back
to the hot stove and get another--
  while the clean, clean bread-scent
of fresh-ironed clothes
  yeasts us into a rising,
you and I.

I use those old irons
   for bookends now.

CHURNING
&

I remember carefully carrying
the sterilized glass churn
up to the separator room
to get the rich new milk poured in.
I thought it a privilege
to be allowed to do the daily churning.
Sitting on the kitchen floor,

with the churn held tightly
between my outstretched legs,
I turned the handle
fast, then slow, then fast again
and watched the wooden
dashers
agitate the white, white milk.
The churn grew warm
from the heat of my legs
and I from the heat
of my efforts.
For a long time there was
little resistance
to the paddles,
and I would always
consider giving up.
Sometimes I sang;
sometimes I counted the
turns
of the handle.
Lulled by the swishing,
by the froth and motion,
the sudden coming of the
butter

was always a surprise--
    at first, small fragments, a hint,
then, all at once, butter--
    unmistakably yellow, heavy,
clinging to the paddles--
    and there was in me
a matching gladness
    that it had happened
to the milk--to me--again.
    It was almost a miracle
to a child, this palpable yellow
    out of liquid white,
and I expected praise
    for making it happen.

    Now, I churn inchoate bits
        of ideas and images
through my white-liquid mind
        and wonder if they
will ever coalesce
        into a poem--
wait for the butter to come.

CANNEL COAL

&

Forever ago
   I took my winter baths
in a galvanized tub set before a coal fire
   in my Grannie's sitting room.
Quiet licking flames heavied my eyes.
   To forestall bed, I begged
my Uncle Joe to put on a piece,
   or even two, of cannel coal--a special treat.
Dried, and hurried into a flannel gown,
   bouncing with anticipation, I was allowed
to place a chunk on all by myself;
   some moments went into the choosing.
It took both hands to pick one up,
   for it was jagged, oily, shiny,
slick, like a just-shed snake.
   It left no black soft-coal dust on my hands.
Immediately it caught and flared,
   adding instant pyrotechnics,
a mini-conflagration, giant sparklers,
   complete with sound-effects.
Our faces, the old Seth Thomas on the mantel,
   the entire room, were suddenly lit up,
and shadows cavorted on the walls
   to the tune of sharp and sassy crackling.
I remember clapping and dancing in the firelight--
   fire-witched, energized, entranced.
"It's candle-coal--a million candles,"
   I sang, stepping back from all the popping.
"Not bi-tu-min-ous, it's an-thra-cite,"
   drawing out the syllables--I loved big words.
"Spats like a feisty woman, just like a feisty woman

throwing a real wild temper tantrum,"
Uncle Joe joked, looking at my mother,
  who didn't deign to answer.
"Then I want to grow up
  to be a *fancy* woman," I declared--
"much more lively (new word)
  than the regular kind!"
"They are," he nodded, laughing hard.
    And I did--
most certainly, indubitably, did.
    Feisty, not *fancy*.

CROPS

&

My grandfather used to swear
　that rocks grew in his fields.
"Might be my finest crop," he said,
and I, a child, believed him.
　Each spring at plowing time
plow blades struck sparks
　on stones not there before
in fields picked clean
　for harrowing and planting.

They harnessed up the mule
　to a slick-iron-runnered sled,
circled through shiny new-turned earth
　harvesting flat limestone slabs.

In slack-time, after rains
　had washed them clean,
my uncle chose proper stones
　judiciously, from great heaps
spring had produced
　and mended his stone fences
or built new ones,
　stacked tight and straight
though mortarless.

　　In fifty years,
　　the fields I've worked
　　have yielded up
　　a less enduring crop.

PATTERNS

You were already old
when I, the youngest grandchild,
   was born, and so I knew you
only in your porch-swing tranquility.
   Now, holding your quilts
in my hands and on my lap,
   I know your patience
and your passion--
   know you by your Bow-Tie,
Double Wedding Ring, Log Cabin,
   Dresden Plate, and Irish Chain,
Starburst, and others
   I cannot name--know you
      by their faded wild abandon
      and your tiny precise stitches.

   And now I see you
in your auburn-haired
   young wifehood,
calling to your children,
   running to gather in your man
returning from the threshing--
   hear your long laugh
at his sweaty rough embrace.
   Now I see your quick
and knowing needle
   and your snapping eyes--
see you on your knees
   laying out your patterns,
      going by the old ones,
         working out your own.

FOR FRANCES

&

It is hard saying goodbye
when you have been part of my life
   all of my life--
closer, really, than family.
   But we have talked about
your being ready to get it over with--
   that your marriage had been special,
that you are proud of your sons and their families
   and that your life over all has been good.
We talked about the crossing over.
   We read old letters and poems
and laughed at old memories.
   We shared so much, you and I--
confidences and books, flowers, and pieced quilts,
   worries, and holidays, and quiet times.
You taught me to "snap my eyes"
   to make my children mind
and how to keep my mouth shut
   when I really wanted to set them straight
and have them do things my way.
   It helped to share them with you.
We talked about basketball, chickens,
   and Democrats, trout lilies and recipes--
about living each day and...dying.
   I wanted to be like you when I grew up,
and when I told you so,
   you laughed your smoke-husky laugh in disbelief.
But though we joked, you knew I meant it.
   You told me that you could never cry
and that you were never lonely.
   So you leave me more than hooked rugs and quilts;

you leave me optimism and courage, always--
  and the great gift of your gladness for my company.

  Now the days are hot and sultry,
and the cicadas you will not hear
  already portend the end of summer.
You and I used to wait for rain,
  remember--and enjoy storms together.
And now corn-flower blue chicory and
  Queen Anne's lace edge the roadways
and corn and tobacco grow day by day
  under the sun and summer showers.
Passing them by, you go to the country cemetery
  to lie next to Clark in that place finally.
But you will not be in the flower-covered coffin,
    Frances--not really, not you.
  You will be striding briskly
    through the tall grass
      of the rolling hills of home.
  Keep watching. I will come.

YOUNGEST CHILD

&

It was always hard
    being the youngest child.
Upstairs in the big feather bed
    with three of my cousins,
I was always on the outside
    where it was coldest
and I had to tug for my share
    of the quilts and the comfort.
We lay together spoon-fashion
    and scratched the back
        in front of us,
then flipped to our other side
    and scratched that back,
which meant that on my right side
    I had no back to scratch,
so I would fall asleep.
I did like being with the older ones
    and listening to their talk.
But then they told
    at the supper table
about my getting up
    in the deep of the night
        to use the slop jar,
(I didn't have to crawl over anyone)
    and my warm sleep-moist bottom
had stuck to the frigid metal rim--
    and I had to call for help.
(I lost some skin anyway.)
    I blushed and ran away
when they told, and everybody laughed,
    first my brother, then my cousin Susan,
then my grandmother, and an uncle--
    even shy Aunt Eleanor.

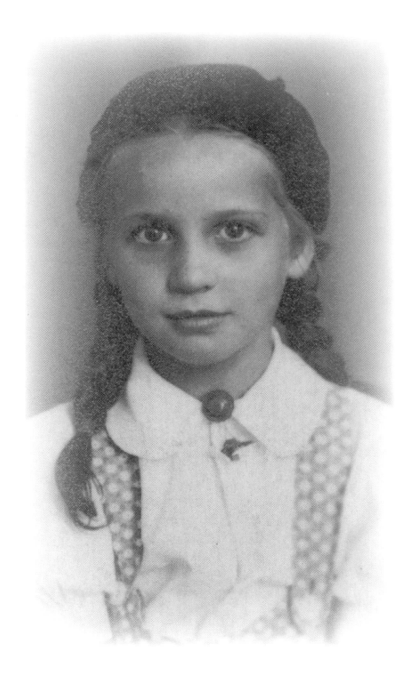

LAST LAP
&

STEPS

I remember
how I used to run
everywhere
and take steps
two at a time
going up,
filled with energy
and *joie d'vivre*.
Now I one-at-a-time them,
both up and down,
humbled by pain
and longing
for release.
But I remember--
I know--
how it feels
to bounce down
the steps,
giving a little skip
on each one.

DON'T SEE ME OLD

You look at me
and see Old
--old woman.

But I am the girl
    who flings long legs
    over the high-jump bar,
    beating the boys.
I am the curve-breaker
    --head of the class.
And a sweater girl.

I am the woman
    who bears four babies
        silently.
I cajol a car-smashed husband
    back to life.
I raise children
    write poems
    keep house.
I teach college students.
I ride a Silver Bullet moped to work
    at the university.
I go skinny-dipping every year
    in a mountain stream in October.
I drive a tractor to bush-hog steep meadows,
    pull haywagons, guide a Gator,
    milk, and try to plow.
I do whatever needs doing for others,
    and keep searching, searching, thinking--always.
I create. I listen. I learn.

I keep on learning.
Don't see me old, boy.
See me
    young inside and interesting,
    well-worn and wise.
Then, if you possibly can,
    see me beautiful and nimble.

But right now I go
      to run down the orchard hill
            with the wind singing in my hair.

CHOOSING A SEAT

When you begin
entering a room
and taking some time
to choose a seat
strategically--
one central enough
to hear and see,
a chair with arms,
(preferably high)
not a couch,
for easy rising--
not too hard
for the bones--
nor too soft
to get out of--
then, my dear,
you can safely
assume,
you have arrived
at that "certain" age.
and will remain there
for an unknown while.

TECHNIQUE

Positioning themselves
carefully in front
of the chosen chair,
the old ladies move
inch by inch
until the backs
of their legs touch,
or nearly.
Then, leaning forward,
and pointing their bottoms
over the chair seat
as far as possible,
they plop down--
squarely on target--
giving a sigh and
a relieved
smile of triumph.
Jestingly, I once called it
the "point and plop."

I can report to you:
I now appreciate
their technique.

WHERE HAS JOY GONE?

Where has joy gone?
　Is it hiding 'round
the near edge of tomorrow
　　or lying wrecked on shoals of yesterday?

I remember joy--
　it used to leap out
at me in morning sunshine
　　and follow me to school.

Where has joy gone?
　Is it shattered now
on jagged peaks of pain
　　or stranded in deserts of despair?

I do remember joy--
　it used to lurk in laughter
and quiver over stones
　　in tumbling water.

Where has joy gone?
　Is it stopped in quagmires
of age and illness
　　and love's necessary losses?

I can remember joy--
　It swam with me in sun-warmed creeks
and frolicked through barefoot fields
　　of childhood's dreams.

I try to remember joy
   and sometimes have a glimpse--
almost a brush-me-by--
   yet we never meet head-on.

Perhaps it waits for autumn's tang
   or down the bend of winter,
or bubbles up in springtime
   or, flirting, shines in summer.
I will remember joy.

HERACLITUS

Old Heraclitus once wrote
   that you cannot step twice
into the same river--
   or something like.
And even if you could,
   the current would eat away
what you were standing on.
   And you can't go back
and un-do or re-do
   something you've said or done.
Nor can you flip forward
   and see beyond that black wall
(or is it a gate?) that is death
   to see what, if anything, is there.

So I find that, most of the time,
   I am paddling with the current,
or, occasionally, when I am feeling
   especially strong, I try to swim upriver,
but not often and not for long.
   I've discovered it's very tiring.
I also have found that aging
   is quite humbling
in almost any way I can think of.

So I have not arrived at a golden shore,
   not that I can rest on.
But, Heraclitus,
         I have become very good
at floating.

TURNINGS

&

My grandmother's clock
  doles out the hours,
and an aging moon
  rules the sky.
I seem to have grown old
  in service to my mother.
I am heavy with caring.

The year is winding down
  like an old clock spring--
    and the century,
      and the milennium.
I feel the turnings.

Dawn will come, I know--
  even if it's a grey dawn, and
I will go outside where I can
  hear only Nature's clock,
and I will search
  for the small green tips
that promise snowdrops soon
    and crocus
      and daffodils.

REGRETS

These days she dwells
   in starched-gingham days,
in golden sunlit days
   of bareback pony rides
and filled egg baskets
   and beaux.
She subsides gently
   into old age
having spent her life
   so as to avoid
   all possible regrets…
and hears the echoes
   of her childhood game
      "step on a crack--
break your mother's back!"
      …cries now and then
over all the cracks she missed.

NURSING HOME

White hair bed-rumpled,
she sits, tiny and hunched,
    clutching the neck
of her yellowed flannel gown,
    white-whiskered chin
thrust forward, chewing
    against the cud
of loose dentures.

In the brittle sepia photographs
she is demure and solemn
    despite dark sultry eyes
and high-piled glossy hair.
    Sailor-suited she yearns
up at her tall sailor boy,
    or, giggling, embraces
middied waists of schoolgirl friends.

Now, in her silenced world
she fingers absent pearls
    and watches the wind
sway winter branches
    while she wades barefoot
in home's sun-warmed
    shallow summer creek
    and squeals at crawdads
    nibbling at her toes.

DRIED FLOWERS

&

They are gathered together
   three times each day
by the ringing
   of the bell.
They cluster outside
   the dining room
for the three daily
   rituals of food.
From their separate rooms,
   shuffling down the long halls
on canes and walkers,
   they come together
before the doors are opened.

They are like bunches of dried flowers,
   withered, papery, faded.
They pat their hair
   and smooth their dresses
and shout at each other--
   or sit silently with hands in laps,
thinking of other times and other faces.
   Today there are only nineteen
in the rocking chairs
   and on the benches.
The twentieth was carried out
   only yesterday.
   But the rest have gathered
at the appointed hour
   to wait for the doors
      to open.

SLEEP

Come get me, Sleep,
I am ready.
I will show you:
now I lay me
  down
    down
      down
to sleep.
I pray the Lord –
if there is a Lord –
my soul –
if I have a soul-- to
  keep
    keep
      keep.
If I should die
before I wake,
I pray the Lord –
nevertheless –
my soul
to take –
    take,
      take,
  regardless –
forever.

Wait!
  Wait!
I have things to do.

READY

&

I'm tired, she says,
and cries a little.
   I hold her white head
against my breast.
   She's been telling me
for some time now that
   she is ready to go.
She tells me again that
   where she lives is nice,
the ladies at her table
   are all nice,
the food is good
  and there are flowers
     on the table.
I have so much time, she says;
   I wish I could give you some.
I wish you could, too--I need it.
   But then I don't really feel
      up to doing anything.
I read the newspaper
   and clean out my desk drawers
and look at my old photographs
   and read Charles's love letters again.
They were such good letters, she says,
   and we had good years together,
lots of trips, and Ann.
   Her voice runs down,
      and I hold her hand.
It's getting to be spring, I say,
   and you will feel stronger.
She doesn't hear.

I hold her chilly hand,
light and papery
    in my full-fleshed warm one
and know that she would
    be gone if she could,
and I would let her go
        if I could.

RECOGNIZING

&

She lies curled
  on her left side,
her back to me,
  as she always is.
She startles
  as I touch her arm.
    Mother, I say,
    It's Barbara.
    I'm here with you.
But she is alone--
  more than deaf alone--
alone somewhere
    in a place
that neither of us
    knows.
I lift her covers
  and see her gaunt old bones,
her clean diaper,
  the pillow between her knees.
She hasn't eaten now
  for more than a week.
Yesterday I sucked water
  up into a straw
and released it into her mouth
  She shook her head
and spat it out.
  She's still in there somewhere,
    I think.
I watch her breathe,
  softly, easily.

She must have shifted to her right side
   when she was spooned
into my Dad's embrace.
   I would tiptoe
into their room
   to watch them sleep,
wanting his arm
   around me, too.
Sometimes I snuggled
   in between them
but then she always stirred
   and soon got up
and left us to start her day.

Now I move to the other side
   of the bed,
watching her sleep,
   thinking: no fear,
no pain
   but wishing
      wishing
she would open her eyes
   recognize me,
her only child--
   maybe even be glad
      I am here--
         know that she won't.
Know that she never was.

OLD LOVERS

&

Tall old lovers
   lean together as they walk,
arms and hands braided tight.
   Gray heads almost touching,
they learn each other
   minute by minute.
They smile, watch, listen;
   they unlearn loneliness.
No need for youthful expectations--
   career ambitions far behind,
the pull of past places, friends, family,
   lost loves, and fears of the future submerged
in contemplation of the new Together,
   they marvel in the long, sweet possibilities
        of Now.
They give each other
   not just memories
but what they have become--
   not what they hope to be,
but what they now are.
   And they are beautiful--
moles, scar lines, laugh creases,
   age spots, wrinkles--all.
No time for might-have-beens,
   used-to-be's, or counting losses,
they plan their new home together
   (dream of playing house)
and hikes and trips, elderhostels,
   and family celebrations
with this new calculus of two.

Old lovers are a new creation,
   and love, their own miracle,
      lights their steps
         and prophesies good to them
            in a long forever.

A Wedding Poem for
Carol Hutcheson and Ben Pickard

EPITAPH

&

So what about this field trip?
   It has been both long and short.
What I am finding out,
   moment by moment,
is how much has been left out—
   early and future and in the middle.
Surely it was more than an experiment,
   though it seems much like
      the preparation
   to get ready to begin.
And I do wonder who designed
      this exercise in living
and what was intended
      to be learned?
The old What is Truth, or Beauty,
or Wisdom, or Virtue, or Love?
      Or is it the Why?

Leave it at this: I am learning
      there is no final word.

EULOGY

&

I would not mind
   being remembered
as a planter of trees,
   a grower of fruit,
      a maker of poems,
   a wind-watcher,
      a friend,
         a lover.

POST SCRIPTS
&

JULY 4, 2007

While I am writing a poem
the tomato's cheek reddens
and the balloon-flower
opens wide its purple lips
as the tiny hidden warbler
flings high its summer song.

While I am writing a poem,
limp flags hang from houses
and the Fourth of July parade
forms up, in the rain, regardless.
All the graves in military cemeteries
are breast-spiked with flags;
they make a gallant show.

While I am writing a poem,
coneflowers toss bright tousled heads;
daisies lift their faces to the sun,
and brazen chipmunks
chase each other through the grass.
Now a goldfinch flashes across.
High summer in Kentucky.

While I am writing a poem,
five American soldiers are blown to bits
in their Humvee in dusty Anbar Province,
and a truck bomb explodes near the Green Zone.
Only fifty-five civilians are killed,
with countless wounded, red splashing a brown land.
Hooded Hamas has taken over the Gaza Strip,
where water and electricity are missing.

While I am writing a poem,
the President commutes a sentence
and makes a speech honoring the brave dead,
with the flag behind, in the background.
He vows again to stay the course.
But nothing of renditions, Abu Graib, or Guantanamo.
Another Shiite mosque in Baghdad is destroyed.
And now the British are on high alert.
It is Independence Day in America.

While I am writing a poem.

VEGETABLE SOUP

❧

*I*t is hard to begin at the beginning. It was a hot day in late July, at the very end of the thirties and long before air conditioning. The shades were down on the south side of the house, and the windows thrown wide open on the north and west sides, but still it was miserably hot both inside and outside. Dispositions were fraying, but life had to go on. Which meant that we usually ate our "dinner" at noon, and that was a hot meal--with left-overs or cold-cuts and slaw in the evening, when it was much cooler. Illogical? Probably, but a time-honored tradition in our home, and this day it was to be vegetable soup.

The summer vegetables were begging to be used, and Mother had a soup bone and a chunk of stew beef to throw in. She had spent the morning peeling, cutting, and dicing, but she had been distracted for at least an hour by a neighbor's visit, so she decided to shorten the cooking by putting everything into the big pressure cooker. It presently was hissing and rattling away on the gas stove, the heavy steel pressure gauge jiggling lazily on the top as it mysteriously let the steam out in short or prolonged squirts. The kitchen smelled rich and promising, and the corn dodgers were in the oven slowly baking. The kitchen must have been easily 98 degrees, and the walls were moist with steam.

Remembering, I think it must surely have been a Saturday, because my father was out puttering around in his garage workshop and pestering my mother as to "how much longer?" He was always hungry. My mother was ignoring him as best she could. She had spent the day before, hot as it was, washing down the rough-surfaced kitchen walls and ceiling with Spic-and-Span. She wiped off the cabinets, too, and I did the woodwork and windows--to earn my allowance, as she put it. She had mopped the linoleum early this morning before she began on the vegetables, warning my Dad not to track dirt and sawdust in from the shop. While the soup finished, she went to take a cool bath--which normally she did when she first got up. But the mopping had taken precedence that morning.

I was sitting at the porcelain-topped table reading--as usual, Mother would have said--when my father came in from the shop and went over to the sink to wash up. His coveralls were sweaty, but he had carefully brushed off the sawdust. "I'm famished!" he said for the twentieth time. "MUST be ready!" He grinned conspiratorially at me. I agreed but went on reading. Knowing now how things went, I wish I had watched. I missed a lot. The next thing I heard was a long hiss of steam, a sort of screeching sound, and, shortly thereafter, a large and rather juicy-sounding explosion. My Dad was yelping, and I felt a few hot splatters myself as I tried to adjust to the new landscape of the kitchen.

My Dad--I know now--had wrestled the top off the pressure cooker without letting the steam fully escape, in spite of the tension and the clinging, protesting rubber gaskets--how he did it is still a family mystery. Now vegetable soup was hanging in long strands from the ceiling, was running down the walls, was mounding all over the stove and the floor around it, down into the other burners, was dripping into the grill of the heat duct, had splattered the clean curtains, and decorated my Dad, especially his bald head, from top to toe. He hardly noticed that he was burned, for his overwhelming consternation at the indescribable dispersion of the soup and the undoubted consequences of his impatience were all he could take in for now. He was holding up his hands to catch some of the long ropey mess splatting down from the ceiling, almost in an attitude of supplication. With a reputation as an inveterate wit and something of a comic, he was speechless.

At this point, some seconds into the disaster, my mother arrived, wrapped in a towel, still wet--having heard the explosion in the bathroom even over the noise of the running water. She too was completely overwhelmed, disbelieving, and totally furious. As she took it in and realized the extent of the carnage, she screamed at us, but mostly at my Dad: "OUT! GET OUT!" and burst into tears. We left, I grabbing my book, and my Dad stripping vegetable soup off his arms as he went. The sight of my mother, standing stark naked in what had minutes earlier been her immaculate kitchen, towel unnoticed on the floor, is, to this day, both unforgettable and unbelievable.

At this point my memory ends. I do not remember how badly my father was burned, or how the kitchen got cleaned up, or how long it took my mother to forgive him or the penance she exacted. I don't know if we ever had anything to eat that day, or if we went to bed that night in the same house. I don't even remember where either of us went to hide out. But I do remember that it seemed as if one pressure cooker full of vegetable soup could easily have fed the five thousand--there was so much of it--and I do remember the horrified look on my Dad's face--the face with the soup running down it--and his upthrust hands as my mother appeared in the door, then the lowered hands with palms spread as if he were pleading with her to believe that he had no idea how it had happened and wasn't she worried if he were badly burned. And the "OUT!" rings clearly down the decades.

SLEDDING

&

"Why don't I have brothers and sisters? I'm the only one." I asked, or complained, looking out the window at the mostly gray sky. Not that I expected an answer, for on previous askings, I had usually been ignored. Only once had my mother answered and then tersely,

"Because I wouldn't go through *that* again."

I was feeling let-down and abandoned now that the others had left, and I wanted someone to play with. Usually I didn't mind being an only child, often didn't even remember it, and was used to being left to my own devices.

My aunts, uncles, and cousins had gone home on the Friday morning after Thanksgiving Day--all of them laden with food. That afternoon it started to snow and turned much colder. It snowed all Friday night and part of Saturday. It was a crispy, hard snow, not wet and mushy. Now, whenever the sun peeked through, it made a sparkly snow-blanket. The creek had frozen, and the snow had covered it over, but you could see where it was. Mother said I was not to try to slide on the creek until she could decide how thick the ice was and whether it was safe. Running water frozen over was tricky. I had discovered that for myself the hard way.

Although I was restless and a little lonely, I really didn't mind about not being able to slide on the creek, because I had asked Daddy to bring me my new Flexible Flyer this time when he came up from Knoxville. I had had it for nearly a year but had used it only once. It was a long sled with red runners and red stripes on the wooden part. I had sanded the paint off the runners last winter, but on that Saturday morning I sanded them again and started waxing them with a chunk of the paraffin that Grannie used to seal her canning jars. As I rubbed the paraffin along the bottoms of the runners, I tried to decide which hill was best. I discussed this critical choice with anyone who would listen, with the expectation that my enthusiasm would soon find me a sledding buddy. Uncle Joe had been out all morning milking and feeding, and Daddy had helped in the kitchen and had refilled the coal bin outside the kitchen door. There was a cannel coal fire in the front room crackling and popping and shooting colored flames like small fireworks. I watched it through the kitchen door, my thoughts on swooping down the slopes on my Flexible Flyer. Mother had already told me that wherever I chose, I would need to have a grown-up with me. Since he was my usual playmate when he was not off working, I first asked Daddy to go with me, but he was deep in a Popular Mechanics and was enjoying an unusual chance to rest. So I didn't beg. Uncle Joe didn't want to go out in the cold again. Then Mother quite unexpectedly said she would go with me after an early supper if I would go out and play by myself for a while and not pester anyone.

"Some of us have work to do," she said, "after a holiday."

It was cloudy and looked like snow again, but I went out and played on top of the root cellar for a while--slid down in one of Grannie's big metal dishpans, climbing back up over and over. Finally I built a low snow fort on top and began to stockpile snowballs just in case of an attack. About the time I decided my toes were going to fall off, Mother called me in for fried chicken and gravy, slaw and canned green beans, and biscuits with damson plum preserves--my favorite meal. I had expected leftovers from Thanksgiving, but I now figured out that most of the remains of that meal had gone home with my cousins. I liked this one better anyway; I was just afraid I would be too full to go sledding. Everyone seemed a little tired and content to be inside where it was cozy and warm. But although my mind was outside in the dark, I didn't think to ask Mother which hill we'd try. There was some jam cake left from the day before, but we decided it would taste better afterwards. Grannie said she would do up the dishes and have hot chocolate waiting for us when we came back.

It was full dark, with some clouds and a few stars showing when we started off. We were bundled into the heaviest clothes we could find. Mother had on a pair of Uncle Joe's old corduroy pants and his hunting boots and jacket. I did not remember seeing her in pants before, and I had never seen her in a bathing suit. In fact, my mother seldom played anything with me. She believed children should be able to entertain themselves. So this was a special occasion for both of us. My Dad offered to come with us, then had thoughtfully withdrawn. I knew he was thinking that this was a fine time for us to be together doing something fun. I was hoping she was as excited and eager as I was. I could hardly wait until we had at last collected the sled and our mittens and knit caps from the back porch and actually started off. I was hopping up and down like a jackrabbit but trying not to get off on the wrong foot with Mother and mess things up as I often did. Mother said I had better save my energy as we started down the long gravel driveway toward the front gate.

"Where are we going?" I asked. "The good hills are behind the house. Tell me where...please!"

"You'll see," was all she would say as she plodded through the snow pulling the sled. We went through the gate that Uncle Joe had left open down at the pike and then across the bridge, crossed the road, and stopped before a four-strand barbed wire fence on the far side of the road opposite our front pasture. The ridge we faced seemed to rise straight up. The sky was a little lighter, and everything was bright because of the snow, but this ridge was steeper and higher than anything on our farm. It looked very black against the sky. And I knew this was someone else's land. The hill was too steep for crops, and I had never seen animals on it. Too steep even for animals?

"Mom!" I exclaimed. "Not this hill? There's no place at the bottom to stop. We'll run into the fence!"

"This is the best one," she said. "You'll see. Come on, now--over or under?"

She stretched the bottom two strands of the wire apart, and I slipped through, then held them for her as the followed. We held the lowest strand up high enough to pull the sled under, then started the long climb to the top. It was hard keeping our feet--it was steep and slick and heavy-going in the snow. At the top we sat down on the sled to get our breath. Then we saw the nearly-full moon coming up. Looking down, I could now see the pale path of the road beyond the fence that I knew was there. I was deep-down scared, but I didn't want my mother to know I was scared. I wondered what my older cousins would be feeling, waiting at the top of this hill in the moonlight, not knowing, as I was now.

"Ready?" she asked and stood up.

"Yes, I think so," I answered. "But how will we stop?"

"Trust me," she said and lay down on the sled. I lay on my stomach on top of her and held on tightly. I could have used some reassurance just then. We sank down a little, but this snow was perfect for sledding. So it took only a little push with her hands before we were flying down the hill with wind and snow in our faces. It didn't seem as if we even touched the snow. We actually could have been airborne! I was terrified, but it felt like all the dreams I had ever had of speed and flying. My face stung; my eyes watered. I felt like loosening my arms from around her shoulders and taking off into the sky. Then my mother yelled, "Get ready!" Just as the dark wires of the fence were visible, she rolled us off the sled into the snow, and the sled dug in and stopped right at the fence. She just lay in the snow laughing. I couldn't believe my own mother. I was still gasping for breath--but relieved, excited, exhilarated. We lay there laughing in the moon-struck November night like two kids.

We trudged up that hill three more times and flew down. My legs grew heavier and heavier climbing up, but the thrill of that downward flight kept me going. My heart almost stopped every time we neared the bottom and our rough "dismount." The fear was there each trip. Then, too tired to make the climb again, we turned, snow-covered and cold, toward our lighted windows. I asked my mother how she knew what to do on that sledding hill. I was confident that she didn't like to take chances. She was always telling my Dad not to take risks. Like cutting his fingers off with his table saw.

"Jimmy and I did this once or twice--twice, I guess--years ago, when he was courting me."

"Courting you? A Jimmy?"

"He was my beau before your Daddy," she explained. "He had a lot of money for a young man, and he thought I was going to marry him. But then I met your Daddy in Louisville, where I was teaching fifth grade, and that was that. Jimmy gave me my platinum bar-pin with the diamond--you've seen it--but he wouldn't take it back. Jimmy Adams was his name, and I thought I loved him for a while." All this was new to me; my mother never talked about personal things. I thought this felt kind of good, but I didn't want to push my luck by asking too much.

"And Jimmy took you sledding on that hill? Didn't you wonder if he wanted to kill you off or something?"

"No. But your Grannie thought it was wicked! I was lying on top of him."

"Not wicked," I said, "Just dangerous." And we looked at each other in the moonlight and grinned. She reached out and grabbed hold of the sled's rope, and we pulled it home together.

EMERGENCIES
&

As far as I have been able to ascertain, my mother was never good at emergencies. I discovered that fact for myself as a child and was not surprised to hear it mentioned, though not fully specified, by her brothers and sisters. One of the occasions that comes to mind is the beautiful summer day that I was helping with the washing. We had a wringer washing machine--a prized possession--on the back porch. I could do most of the washing myself and took pride in being allowed to do so. I was washing a load of sheets, pillow cases and towels. I liked to see them swished round and round in the sudsy water, liked to see the water pumped out into the concrete wash tubs nearby. We used that soapy water to soak the dirtier things--usually my Dad's work clothes-- before putting them into the washer. I liked to see the sheets turn whiter during the second rinse when the soapy water was flushed away. But the wringing out through the big rubber rollers was the part I liked best. I knew how to pull the sheets out of the washer and put a corner in between the rollers, help guide it through until it fell into the clean, lined basket positioned to catch them.

On this day, my concentration must have slipped, because, just after I fed the corner of the sheet in and it caught between the rollers, I found the fingers of my left hand caught with the sheet. My right hand almost followed, but I jerked it back in time. At first I tried to resist, but pulling back was very painful. I yelled for Mom. She did not respond at once, so I screamed, "Hurry!" The rollers rolled inexorably on. When my elbow passed between them, I nearly fainted with pain. Mother arrived at this point. "Stop it!" I begged. She was paralyzed. "Stop it," I screamed. It would soon be up to my armpit. I tried to reach across myself to hit the roller release button, but I couldn't reach it. "Mother!" Finally, she reached out, almost in a dream state and turned the knob to reverse. Slowly, inch by quarter inch my arm was processed back through the roller. I was crying with pain. It was excruciating, but I knew now that my arm would not be ripped off. It was blue, very blue. When finally my fingers were released, I found I could not bend my arm at all; I cradled it across my chest. My mother stood beside me, still speechless, still paralyzed with fright. I went to the kitchen sink and filled it with hot water. Since I couldn't bend the arm, I couldn't get it immersed up to the elbow, so I went to the bathroom, filled the tub and got myself in, clothes and all. My mother followed to watch. "Are you all right?" she finally asked. "I don't know," I answered, swamped with pain.

By the end of the summer, my arm was almost back to normal, except for the elbow, which didn't want to bend and did so protestingly. I had strange linear marks up and down my arm for many months. I don't remember when they went away. I was never taken to the doctor, of course. My mother didn't believe in spending money on doctors. Never ill herself, she felt that most things would heal themselves, given enough time--and they usually did. We were really lucky to be healthy, since we had so little money. I doubt she would have made check-ups or regular visits even if we had been wealthy. As I say, we fortunately were amazingly healthy—at least as long as I lived at home and she was in charge. Maybe ill-health was scared out of us. It is possible, I suppose.